The GREAT COMPROMISE

The GREAT COMPROMISE

GREG LAURIE

This Billy Graham Evangelistic Association special edition is published with permission from FM Management.

WORLD WIDE PUBLICATIONS
Minneapolis, Minnesota 55403

Unless otherwise noted, Scripture quotations are from The New King James Version. Copyright © 1979, 1980, 1982, Thomas Nelson, Inc., Publisher.

Scriptures marked KJV are from The King James Version of the Bible.

Scriptures marked NIV are from The Holy Bible, New International Version. Copyright © 1973, 1978, 1984 International Bible Society. Used by permission of Zondervan Bible Publishers.

Scriptures marked AMP are from The Amplified Bible. Copyright © 1965 Zondervan Publishing House. Used by permission.

Scriptures marked PHILLIPS are from the New Testament in Modern English by J. B. Phillips, published by Macmillan Company, © 1958, 1960, 1972 by J. B. Phillips. Used by permission.

Library of Congress Cataloging-in-Publication Data:

Laurie, Greg
    The great compromise/Greg Laurie
      p. cm.
    ISBN 0-913367-31-1
    (previously published by Word Publishing, ISBN 0-8499-1141-9)
    1. Christian life.   2. Spiritual warfare.   I. Title.

Printed in the United States of America.

Contents

To the bride of my youth,
best friend and counselor—Catherine. . . .

Acknowledgments

I would like to thank all those involved in the preparation of this book:

Karen Dagher, for her help in adapting the original messages and in helping with the framework of the book;

Alyse Lounsberry for determination and creativity in helping to shape it;

And all my new friends at Word Publishing who have made the writing of this book a wonderful experience.

I wish to thank Kip Jordon for catching the vision to bring my messages through the written word as well as from the pulpit;

Also special thanks to Byron Williamson, David Moberg, Joey Paul, and Susan Ligon.

Finally, thanks to David Riley for his artistic input and design; special thanks to Rolf Zettersten for his friendship and foresight; and an excellent staff of associates at Harvest Christian Fellowship including Paul, John, and Carol and, of course, the wonderful flock of believers that I have had the privilege of pastoring for twenty-two years.

Prologue

Do you remember when you first met Jesus Christ? Are you as impassioned now as you were then? Think back for a minute to the day you first realized how empty you were inside—and you finally admitted you *needed* something. Then you heard about Jesus Christ and how He could forgive you and make you a new person on the inside. Because the Holy Spirit was nudging at your heart, it became clear to you that only Jesus could fill that deep void inside you. So you invited Him into your heart. It felt good not to be empty any longer, didn't it?

But wait a minute! In a few days, your old buddies began to tug at you, nagging you to go out for a beer. "Just one!" your very best buddy urges. "No!" the voice of your conscience counters. "Why not?" your buddy persists. "Are you all of a sudden some religious *fanatic?*"

Now, that one gets to you, doesn't it? *You—a religious fanatic?* You must be kidding! No way! You certainly don't want to give *that* impression. Somewhere along the way, to avoid picking up an unsavory label like *that one,* you make a subtle compromise—just a *little one!* You determine that in order to win your buddies to Jesus, you'll just have to hang around them, blend in, gain their confidence, and just be one of the gang. You decide that once they feel comfortable with the "Christian" side of you, you'll tell them about Jesus a little at a time—nothing too heavy. No preaching. Eventually they'll have to see it your way. Remember?

I know you meant it when you invited Jesus Christ into your heart. But I also know how alluring the world and all it has to offer can be. When did it happen? When did the world begin to choke out your Christian walk? Was it about the time you began mowing the lawn on Sundays instead of going to church? Was it when you decided that instead of tithing, you should invest that money in a high-yield money market account? Was it when you started smoking again? Or when you determined that you and your wife should get a divorce because of "irreconcilable differences?" Was it when you became more interested in what was showing at the movies than what was happening at your church? Or when you spent weekends pursuing leisure activities, and found a new love interest?

One day you wake up and realize how miserable you are. There's that old, familiar emptiness again. You feel defeated on the inside, and on the outside—on most days—you are barely able to keep it together. Deep down inside, you feel it's too late to change. You blew it. What would Jesus want with a loser like you?

Is that how it is? Then this book is written just for you.

Perhaps you have been faithfully serving Jesus for many years. Granted, life has become a little boring lately. You have begun to wonder what it would be like if you just let your guard down a little bit—just a little—in this or that area. You wonder what it would be like to just cast off a few restraints. You haven't actually *done* anything about it yet, but you're thinking about it. Thinking about it a lot. Daydreaming about it. Looking for an opening . . . *any opening.* Whether you know it or not, you're a prime target for the devil, who's been waiting patiently for just the right opportunity to take you down. He's been setting you up for a long time for just such a fall.

Is that how it is? Then this book is just for you.

But let's say you are a strong Christian—everybody says so—and you have even personally led many people to Jesus Christ. Of course, you're not perfect and you know it. God knows it. (The devil knows it too.) Surely *you* don't need to read a book like *The Great Compromise!* Whether you know it or not, you may be in the most serious danger of flaming out spiritually. The Bible says, "Therefore let him who thinks he stands take heed lest he fall" (1 Cor. 10:12).

Is that how it is? Then this book is most of all for you.

In each of these scenarios, there is a common denominator. *Compromise.* Sounds relatively harmless, doesn't it? But don't be deceived. Compromise is a Christian's deadliest enemy. Take my word for it. I have met many Christians who fell by the wayside, but I have never met a single one who fell all at once. In each case, the individuals let their guards down, one small compromise at a time. Eventually all those little compromises added up to create one big one—the *great compromise*. That's the one they couldn't pull out of—the one that eventually took them down.

Clearly, compromise is one of the greatest dangers confronting today's Christians. My reason for writing *The Great Compromise* is to help Christians in the 90s learn how to spot compromise—and stamp it out.

Compromise—clever, seductive, subtle, deadly—is one of the most effective tactics ever invented by the devil for use against Christians. Satan really doesn't expect to convince most Christians to go out and commit some horrendous sin. No, he would much rather convince us to lower our guard just a little at a time— so gradually that we hardly realize it when we stumble. Instead of falling headlong into a pattern of sin, we drop our standards one notch at a time until our integrity is impaired, our character is endangered, and our relationship with God is damaged.

Christian writer Graham Scroggie once said that compromise prompts us to be silent when we ought to speak up for fear of offending; it prompts us to praise when it is not deserved to keep people our friends; and it prompts us to tolerate sin and not to speak out because to do so might give us enemies.[1]

Yes, compromise is a powerful and effective tool in the hands of our adversary, the devil. Jesus recognized how subtle and potentially dangerous this particular tactic can be—and even based two parables on it. So why don't we hear more about compromise today? Could it be that we are not being properly instructed about its potential destructiveness? Why are Christians not being warned of its subtle erosive influences?

Consider the story of a massive redwood tree that had survived some 400 years in one of America's national forests. This ancient tree had survived fourteen separate strikes by lightning. It had survived countless earthquakes, storms, floods, and other violent natural disasters. Yet one day, without warning, this massive, towering old tree came crashing to the ground with a tremendous thud! No bolt of lightning was responsible. No overzealous lumberjack had felled it. It just came crashing to earth for no apparent reason.

On closer inspection, investigators discovered why this old tree had died. Tiny beetles had found their way inside its trunk and had begun eating away at its life-giving fibers, weakening its mighty bulk from the inside out. Just imagine—what many lightning bolts, horrendous storms, and earthquakes could not do was easily accomplished over the passage of time by a handful of small insects!

In much the same way, the devil tries to bring down Christians through a steady drone of small, seemingly insignificant temptations. While we are fighting and resisting him in one area, we may be setting up house with him in another area of our lives. Just as those small beetles found access to the tender core of a huge, 400-year-old redwood, Satan will find ways to creep into our lives for the purpose of eroding our foundations until our fibers have become undone and we come crashing to the ground.

Show me a person who has fallen away from their walk with the Lord and I will show you a person who started making compromises in his or her life long ago. It's rare to find someone who is walking with the Lord one day and then completely abandons Him the next day. In fact, I maintain that it just doesn't happen that way—ever! I can almost guarantee that when this type of drastic change takes place, the individual in question has made compromise after compromise after compromise until the inevitable end result—falling away—finally took place. That's why we as Christians must be careful not to compromise.

Our Jewish friends know the dangers of compromise. Jewish tradition warns of compromise. As part of their Passover celebration, Jewish people still go through their houses annually to remove all items containing leaven, or yeast. The Old Testament identifies leaven as a symbol of sin. With that in mind, Paul wrote to the church at Corinth regarding their welcoming immoral persons into their fellowship: "Your glorying is not good. Do you not know that a little leaven leavens the whole lump? [Or a little yeast works through the whole batch of dough?] Therefore purge out the old leaven, that you may be a new lump" (1 Cor. 5:6–7).

As we look at the Church today, it is important to realize that wherever God is working, the devil is also present to oppose. Whenever God's people say, "Let us rise up and build," the devil and his workers are right there, saying, "Let us rise up and oppose them." That's why, in order to win, we must engage in warfare. There is no progression without opposition. There is no winning without warfare. For that reason, we must brace ourselves against attack and at all times keep our guards up.

Perhaps each of us could benefit from a little spiritual house-cleaning. Could we not each benefit from asking ourselves, "Is there any compromise in my life today? Is there something that is choking out my spiritual strength, draining me of zeal, and leavening my life?" Now is a good time to deal with the issues that compromise our Christian walks.

If we don't stop and deal with this dangerous thing called compromise, we may wind up felled one day like that giant, 400-year-old redwood—undone from within by subtle, seemingly insignificant forces we identified as nuisances that were in fact threatening our very spiritual lives.

As you read this book, I hope you will prayerfully ask the Lord to show you any areas of compromise that may exist in your life, areas of "leaven" that unwittingly may be hindering your relationship with Him. You may even pray, as did the psalmist, "Search me, O God, and know my heart; Try me, and know my anxieties; And see if there is any wicked way in me, And lead me in the way everlasting" (Ps. 139:23).

My prayer for you is that the Holy Spirit will shine His powerful light through your heart, showing you any area that should be dealt with, and even inspiring you to pray to rid yourself of any "leaven." Then you can start shoring up those weaknesses so you may be strong in the day of the devil's attacks and able to resist the subtle compromises that he daily sends your way. Finally, it is my hope that reading *The Great Compromise* will help you to recapture any zeal for the Lord that you may have lost along the way.

Compromise is subtle. It's dangerous—even deadly! But in order to effectively use this tactic, the devil must work in secrecy. Once you begin to understand how compromise works, it will change your spiritual life!

PART 1

THE FORCE
OF COMPROMISE

1

GIVING GOD A MAKEOVER

And the rest of it he makes into a god, his carved image. He falls down before it and worships it, prays to it and says, "Deliver me, for you are my god."

—Isaiah 44:17

I believe that even the casual observer will admit that we are living in the last days—days of great uncertainty and danger. It doesn't take a rocket scientist to figure that out. All around us, we see signs that Jesus and the Hebrew prophets warned would mark these end times. Before our very eyes, these age-old biblical prophecies are coming to pass. One can hardly pick up a newspaper or watch a television news program without finding some world headline that fits in perfectly with fulfillment of end-time Bible prophecies.

One thing the Bible says will mark the end times is a great falling away from the faith. The Bible calls this *apostasy*. I maintain that apostasy is something that doesn't happen overnight. It happens over an extended period of time, as a person's faith becomes eroded, weakened, damaged, then destroyed.

In 1 Timothy, chapter 4, the apostle Paul warned believers about times like these: "The Spirit clearly says that in later times some will abandon the faith and follow deceiving spirits and things taught by demons. Such teachings come through hypocritical liars, whose consciences have been seared as with a hot iron. . . . If you point these things out to the brothers, you will be a good minister of Christ Jesus, brought up in the truths of the faith and of the good teaching that you have followed" (vv. 1, 2, 6, NIV).

The Bible warned that these end times would be satanically energized. Our adversary, the devil, is clever. He has been doing what he does for centuries. He's good at it. In fact, the devil is stepping up his efforts against mankind in these last days. The reason he is working so feverishly to take believers down is that he knows his days are numbered and his eternal fate is sealed.

First Corinthians, chapter 10, contains a list of several snares and pitfalls that the devil used hundreds of years ago to take the Israelites down during their wilderness journey—which was meant to be short but lasted forty years. These pitfalls worked on the Israelites then and, ironically, they are the same ones the devil uses today to undermine the faith walks of believers. These clever pitfalls kept all but two of an entire generation number-ing nearly three million souls out of the Promised Land. They continue to present real stumbling blocks in the lives of Chris-tians in the 90s. But today, we call them "compromises."

The devil is diligently at work in this generation, using essen-tially the same tactics that he used against the Israelites, just dressed up in contemporary terminology. He knows exactly what buttons to push to catch us off guard. He knows how to make the world and all it offers seem glamorous and attractive. He knows exactly how to attempt to convince us that Jesus will not return any time soon. He knows what it takes to divert our attentions elsewhere. Then one day we wake up to discover that our original zeal for God has been replaced with some luke-warm, poor excuse for it.

The devil even knows how to convince us that it's OK to com-promise. He and his demonic army have been working for centuries to make sin seem palatable. He's good at taking the edge off the conviction of the Holy Spirit. He's good at mak-ing God seem less than who He actually is—sovereign Lord. He's good at making God seem modern, updated to suit the times, an understanding, "user-friendly" God who looks the other way when we decide to bend or break a few of His com-mands.

God in Our Image

The French philosopher Voltaire once wrote, "God made man in His image, and man returned the favor."

Ever since the perfect image of God was ruined when sin entered the Garden of Eden, mankind has been attempting to recreate God in his own frail image. Being incurably religious, we want a God we can comprehend in neat, finite, human terms. We want a God we can understand—a "designer" deity, if you will. We want a God we can predict and figure out. We want a deity we can control. We want a deity custom-made to suit our individual needs and circumstances. We want a God who will put up with our mood swings and temper tantrums. We want a God we can check in with now and then, a God who will tolerate our excesses and oversights, One who will love us right where we are and look the other way when we fail or refuse to live up to clearly defined biblical standards. We want "Religion Lite."

In the 90s there is a trend toward increasing one's self-esteem. Consequently, we seem to be searching for a God who will help us feel OK about ourselves. We want "feel good" religion, but what about conviction of sin? When the conviction of the Holy Spirit begins to work within a person's life, it doesn't necessarily feel good, does it?

All this reminds me of "The Temple of the Thousand Buddhas," an unusual place of worship in Kyoto, Japan, where worshipers can literally design their own deity. The temple is filled with more than a thousand likenesses of Buddha—each one a little different from the next. Worshipers can pick and choose which they like best. Devotees of Buddha often try to find the likeness they feel most resembles themselves. Then they bow before it in worship. Isn't this a bit like many church goers in the 90s whose search for "quick-fix" religion often ends in compromise?

Slowly but surely, we have given God a "90s makeover." At the expense of reverence for His sovereignty, we have made God over into a comfortable pal, a "user-friendly" God who makes allowances for our sin and excuses for our backgrounds—a non-judgmental God who will easily adapt to our chosen lifestyles and give us "brownie points" for doing a good turn now and then. We have made God over into a deity who delights in the small amounts of attention we choose to give—One who happily rewards us for attending church when we feel like it. We even view Him as approving when we make biblically indefensible statements like, "I don't believe in a God of judgment!" or "The God I follow would never allow suffering or condemn my chosen lifestyle!"

To individuals who actually believe statements like those, I say, "It's time to wake up!" God's Word repeatedly reminds us that He is the same God today as in the beginning. He is "the Alpha and the Omega, the Beginning and the End. . . ." (Rev. 1:8). He is the same "yesterday, today, and forever" (Heb. 13:8).

Yet we continue to attempt to reinvent Him. A recent issue of *Life* magazine featured a story in which different people from different walks of life were asked to describe their prayer lives. A prostitute said, "A lot of people think working girls don't have any morals, any religion. But I do. I don't steal. I don't lie. The way I look at it, I'm not sinning. He's not going to judge me. I don't think God judges anybody."[1]

Apparently, this woman's "work" was prostitution. The problem with her approach to religion is that she seems to be picking and choosing the parts of the Bible that appeal to her. She has apparently selected which of God's commandments she wishes to obey, then adapted them to suit her lifestyle. She has conveniently chosen not to acknowledge God's clear guidelines concerning sexual purity and warnings against impurity.

There is a word to describe modifying God's laws in this manner—*idolatry*. When we do this, we are really giving God a makeover. We are making Him into our own image. We will examine this area of compromise in detail in chapter 4.

"Touchy-Feely" Religion

Has the church of the 90s raised a standard to point the way for the unchurched to find Christ and become true believers? I fear not. Instead, the church of the 90s appears to be busy about the task of developing churches which cater to the whims, interests, and desires of the unchurched in hopes that this approach will win them over. What is being depicted to these individuals is a "user-friendly" God who will smile benignly down upon their lifestyles of choice, as they continue to live as they like—while, of course, dutifully attending these churches! But Christianity is not like that. It involves commitment, servanthood, sometimes even sacrifice. Why aren't more of these messages being preached from many of today's pulpits?

In his book, *The Body,* Chuck Colson shared the results of a survey that appeared in *Business Week* magazine. He wrote, "The books selling in Christian bookstores today are the 'touchy-feely' ones that focus on self-esteem, self-fulfillment, and self-analysis, while devotionals and missionary biographies gather dust on the shelves. So do books encouraging self-sacrifice."[2]

Along these same lines, a 1990 *Newsweek* cover story heralded the dramatic religious resurgence among baby boomers with this interesting observation: "Unlike earlier religious revivals, the aim this time is support, not salvation; help rather than holiness; a circle of spiritual equals rather than an authoritative church or guide. A group affirmation of self is at the top of the agenda, which is why some of the least demanding churches are now in the greatest demand."[3]

A 1994 *U.S. News & World Report* cover story on the subject of spirituality noted, "American religion has taken on the aura of pop psychology. Many congregations have multiplied their memberships by going light on theology and offering worshipers a steady diet of sermons and support groups that emphasize personal fulfillment. The hottest selling books offer advice on how to become better parents, spouses, employees, bosses, lovers and friends, how to overcome substance abuse and how to lose weight."[4]

While it isn't wrong in and of itself to address issues like these, it is a grave error to make them the central focus of ministry. In our zeal to acquaint Christians in the 90s with God's attributes of mercy, forgiveness, and love for sinners, have we gone overboard? Why is there not more emphasis on God's attributes of holiness, righteousness, and hatred for sin? Could it be that in our desire to become user friendly, the church has compromised, too, in watering down its teaching and preaching of the Word of God?

Each time we say, "I don't believe in a God who would send people to hell," or "My God would never do thus and so," we are giving God a makeover. We are turning our backs on biblical truths in order to recreate a God who is more to our individual tastes and liking.

Not only do we seek to change God, but we also seek to change His truth. A number of mainline religious denominations have amended their theology to reflect the changes of our declining culture. There is just one word for it: compromise. Over the course of four years, one well-known denomination compiled a report on the subject of sexuality. The report concurred that any relationship that is loving and caring is acceptable to God, whether the union is heterosexual or homosexual, married or singles who opt to live together. The report went on to state that it is the church's "moral imperative" to teenagers to use condoms. Moral imperative? What about abstinence? What about self-control? What about God's Word, which explicitly warns, "Do you not know that the unrighteous will not inherit the kingdom of God? Do not be deceived. Neither fornicators, nor idolaters, nor adulterers, nor homosexuals . . . will inherit the kingdom of God" (1 Cor. 6:9–10). What about Hebrews 13:4, which states, "Marriage is honorable among all, and the bed undefiled; but fornicators and adulterers God will judge"?

Even the question of sexism and God has been broached by the church in recent years. The National Council of Churches felt the Bible was too "sexist," so it determined that it needed to be "degendered" to make it more acceptable to Christians in the 90s. They appointed a committee to update the translation. They gave the complete Bible a makeover! Now their version of the opening of the Lord's Prayer goes like this: "Our Father and Mother who art in heaven. . . ."

In 1992 one popular, mainline denomination felt God should be given some new titles for use in their prayer books. They wanted to update things, so they included references to our Creator such as "Grandfather," "Great Spirit," and "Our Grove of Shelter," as well as describing Him as "like a Baker woman who brings the leaven that causes our hopes to rise."

Give me a break!

A So-Called 'Reformation'

Two thousand women gathered in Minneapolis recently to attend a conference held in conjunction with the World Council of Churches' Decade of Churches in Solidarity. According to an article in *Christianity Today,* some rather strange things went on at this conference. Some who were present referred to this event as the "Second Reformation." But judge for yourself: "During one session, a controversial incantation was used, including the words, 'Our Maker, Sophia, we are women in your image, with the hot blood of our wombs we give form to new life . . . with the nectar between our thighs we invite a lover . . . with our warm body fluids we remind the world of its pleasures and sensations.'"[5]

I don't know how this sounds to you, but to me it sounds more like a gathering of New Age believers than a conference attended by women who call themselves Christians. If this were a New Age gathering, we might consider such a "prayer" to be par for the course. But for Christians?

The article also stated, "Many of the thirty-four major speakers charged that the church and its belief in the incarnation and atonement of Jesus Christ was a patriarchal construct and had caused oppression of women, violence in the streets, child abuse, racism, classism, sexism, and pollution. 'I can no longer worship in a theological context that depicts God as an abusive parent and Jesus as the obedient, trusting child,' Virginia Mollenkott said. 'This violent theology encourages the violence in our streets and nation.'"[6]

But wait! It gets worse. Referring to the atonement, feminist theologian Delores Williams said, "I don't think we need folks hanging crosses and blood dripping and weird stuff." Her Chinese counterpart, Kwok Pui-Lan, claimed, "If we cannot imagine a Jesus as a tree, a river, as wind, and as rain, we are doomed together."[7]

Finally Korean professor Chung Hyun Kyung led the group in trying to "harness" the divine energy of the universe using New Age techniques. Remember, this was at a gathering of Christian denominations. As an apparent substitute for the Lord's Supper, the conference leaders prayed, "Sophia, we celebrate the nourishment of your milk and honey" in an invitation to "the banquet of Creation." [8]

Wait a minute. If this is not giving God a makeover, what is? Is this not a classic example of bending God and the Bible to suit one's own unique belief system? If this is not making God over into one's own image of what He should be, what is?

"User-friendly" Churches

What is happening in the church today? Instead of turning the world upside down with the power of the gospel, as the early church did, we have allowed the world to turn *us* upside down. We have allowed the world to "squeeze us into its mould" (see Rom. 12:2, PHILLIPS).

Granted, some of these examples of how compromise has crept into the modern-day church are somewhat extreme, but what about the many subtle ways in which compromise has penetrated our ranks? No doubt everyone is attracted to the "feel good" qualities of God's love, forgiveness, and compassion—not to mention the incredible "fringe benefit" of eternal salvation. At the same time many are appalled by the idea that this same God who loves us also requires repentance, trust, and a lifestyle of holiness and obedience to His commands. Many in contemporary society seem put off by a God who forgives but also promises to judge all those who fail to come to Him by His own terms.

There it is again. We want to set the terms. We want a "user-friendly" God who will put up with anything and everything in our search for truth.

Many of us have been bombarded with a one-sided, out of balance, distorted caricature of a hostile God in heaven who allegedly delights in punishing sin by tossing people into hell's gaping fires, but this is no excuse for opting to go to the other extreme. Nowhere in the Bible is God depicted as one who will put up with anything and everything and love us through it all. Nowhere does the Bible depict a God who will not allow us to reap the consequences of our actions.

This reminds me of an experience I had in Hawaii several years ago. I was speaking on the island of Oahu, where we have held several of our evangelistic outreaches called Harvest Crusades. One night as I walked down the main drag of Waikiki Beach, I came upon a wild-eyed man who was holding up a large, hand-painted sign which contained the blaring message: "The wages of sin is death!" As he walked back and forth, up and down this busy street packed with tourists and islanders all hurrying to get somewhere, he shouted and screamed at the passersby, telling them in no uncertain terms that they were all going to hell.

Concerned that this man was seriously misrepresenting the gospel message, I approached him and tried to have a conversation with him. I told him that although it was certainly biblically true to say that the wages of sin is death, he might consider using a more balanced message. "Why don't you put the rest of the verse you are quoting on the other side of that placard," I suggested.

"Romans 6:23 says, 'For the wages of sin is death, but the gift of God is eternal life in Christ Jesus our Lord.' That way people will hear both sides of the story. Besides," I added, "the Bible also states that it is the goodness of God that leads us to repentance."

Unfortunately, this very zealous individual wasn't particularly interested in giving a balanced version of the gospel. He was not very receptive to my advice and he shouted that *I* was headed for hell too.

While it is true that this type of distortion does take place today, it is not the most dangerous type of distortion that exists. Quite frankly, I believe the other extreme is even more dangerous and poses much more of a threat to Christians. Recoiling from a negative distortion of an angry God, many have allowed the pendulum of truth to swing too far in the opposite direction. When was the last time you heard a "hellfire and brimstone" message preached? For that matter, when was the last time you even heard a preacher politely mention hell?

No More "Hellfire and Brimstone"

Although it is true that in some of our learning institutions, Jonathan Edwards' famous sermon entitled "Sinners in the Hands of an Angry God" may be admired as great literature, I seriously doubt that Edwards would be welcome to preach such a message in the pulpits of today. I'm certain he would be required to revise it and tone it down somewhat. He probably would be asked to make it more "politically correct." Perhaps once he reworked it for the 90s, he could call it, "People With Low Self-Esteem from Dysfunctional Families in the Hands of an All-Caring, Non-Judgmental Supreme Being."

I fear that in our desire to make our churches more "seeker-sensitive" and "user-friendly," we have watered down the messages delivered from our pulpits. In so doing, we have taken the "teeth" out of the gospel. The pure and simple message of the gospel—that we are sinners, that sin separates us from God, and that Jesus paid the price to reconcile us to God by taking our sins upon Himself on the cross—has dynamic, explosive power. But in our zeal to make the gospel more palatable to the masses, we have stripped it of its clarity and power.

Paul said, "For I am not ashamed of the gospel of Christ, for it is the power of God to salvation for everyone who believes. . . ."

(Rom. 1:16). The word Paul used for "power" in this passage is the Greek word, *dunamis*. From it, our English words "dynamic" and "dynamite" are derived. Yes, there is *explosive* power in the God-inspired, God-breathed gospel message, but not when we change it or update it to suit our own needs in the 90s.

Is it not the object of the Scriptures to transform *us* into God's image—not the other way around? When we begin to tamper with the essentials of the Bible, rename God, even redefine His very nature, we are making a big mistake.

Any so-called gospel that offers forgiveness without repentance or heaven without hell cannot be found in God's Word. It's a counterfeit message—one that is even more dangerous than we may think. Apparently this type of compromise is nothing new. Writing to believers in Galatia, the apostle Paul warned, "I am astonished that you are so quickly deserting the one who called you by the grace of Christ and are turning to a different gospel—which is really no gospel at all. Evidently some people are throwing you into confusion and are trying to pervert the gospel of Christ. But even if we or an angel from heaven should preach a gospel other than the one we preached to you, let him be eternally condemned" (Gal. 1:6–8, NIV).

The great Bible teacher Martin Lloyd-Jones once wrote that people who teach that God is love without teaching that He hates sin are presenting another god—essentially Satan with a mask on.

The Same Old Excuse

As a pastor, I've probably heard just about every excuse there is. Of course, excuses are nothing new. The Bible is filled with them, from the Garden of Eden—when Adam blamed Eve for his decision to eat the forbidden fruit, and Eve in turn blamed the serpent—forward. Evangelist Billy Sunday called an excuse "the skin of a reason stuffed with a lie."

I once heard a story about a man who lost his job because he never got to work on time. The man sued, arguing that he was handicapped by "chronic lateness syndrome"—and won!

An article entitled "Stop That Whining" that appeared in the *Los Angeles Times* stated, "Are you an 'adult child?' a 'co-dependent?' Critics say recovery groups may offer an excuse for bad behavior. The notion that scars etched deep in childhood resurface as negative behavior in adults is under attack from a number of directions. Critics blast 'recovery' and 'co-dependency' as code for self-absorption. They say the recovery movement has failed to make a distinction between understanding inappropriate behavior, and excusing it. They say that labeling problems as diseases reduces the importance of personal responsibility."[9]

Writing in *The American Therapy Networker,* Atlanta psychiatrist Frank Pittman said, "The adult child movement, by declaring practically everyone to be a victim of imperfect parenting and therefore eligible for lifelong, self-absorbed irresponsibility, has trivialized real suffering and made psychic invalids of those who once had a bad day." [10]

Granted, there are those who have truly been victims of unspeakable abuse and wickedness. But so many are using terms like "victim" and "dysfunctional" to excuse their own irresponsible behavior.

In his book, *The Vanishing Conscience,* author John MacArthur also pointed out this problem. He asked the question, "Whatever happened to guilt and responsibility for what we have done?" [11] He cited the story of a man who was shot and paralyzed while committing a burglary in New York. He later sued the store owner who shot him, and recovered damages. His attorney convinced a jury that this man was first of all a victim of society, driven to crime by economic disadvantages. The lawyer claimed that as a result, he was a victim of the insensitivity of the man who shot him. The plaintiff's attorney claimed that due to the store owner's callous disregard for the thief's plight as a victim of society, he would be confined to a wheelchair for the remainder of his life. The jury agreed. The store owner paid the man a large settlement. Several months later the same man—still in his wheelchair—was arrested for trying to commit another armed robbery.

MacArthur maintained that people who are in trouble because they can't deal with their guilt are today referred to therapists, whose task it is to boost their self-image. It seems that ours is now a society that encourages sin but will not tolerate the guilt that sin produces. What a dilemma!

Even Ann Landers, the widely read syndicated columnist who dispenses counsel and advice on every topic there is, has something to say about guilt. "One of the most painful, self-mutilating, time and energy consuming exercises in the human experience is guilt. It can ruin your day—or your week—or your life—if you let it. . . . Remember, guilt is a pollutant, and we don't need any more of it in the world."

Is it true that guilt is a pollutant we don't need in today's world? What about the place of conscience? What about the Holy Spirit's role as the convicter of sin? What about sin, for that matter? Have we given God such a thorough makeover that we have completely removed the element of sin from our theology?

Personally, I think we could use a lot more guilt and responsibility in today's culture. It's as if we, as a nation, have developed an allergic reaction to dealing with the old-fashioned notion of personal responsibility. Not only do we no longer wish to take responsibility for our sins, but now we have even created a new "politically correct" terminology to define them.

Let's Be Politically Correct!

In *The Official Politically Correct Dictionary and Handbook*, authors Henry Beard and Christopher Cerf [12] have offered up a number of entries to define common problems in today's society. The authors have, in effect, redefined sin.

If your problem is laziness, no problem: you won't be called lazy any longer; now you're simply "motivationally dispossessed."

If your problem is addiction to drugs or alcohol, no problem: you won't be called an addict any longer; now you're simply a "substance abuser" or "chemically inconvenienced."

If your problem is dishonesty, no problem: you won't be called dishonest any longer; now you are "ethically disoriented," "morally different," or "differently honest."

If your problem is promiscuity, no problem: you won't be called promiscuous any longer; now you are "sexually active."

If your problem is serial killing, no problem: you won't be called a serial killer any longer; now you are "socially misaligned," or one who has "difficult-to-meet needs."

If your problem is shoplifting, no problem: you won't be called a shoplifter any longer; now you are one who engages in "non-traditional shopping."

If your problem is sexual perversion, no problem: you won't be called a pervert any longer; now you are termed "sexually dysfunctional."

If your problem is that you lean toward sado-masochism, no problem: you won't be called a sado-masochist any longer; now you are simply "differently pleasured."

Using these new definitions, even the Ten Commandments may one day be rewritten to make them more politically correct. Would you care for some examples?

• Instead of "Thou shalt not kill," "You should not be socially misaligned."

• Instead of "Thou shalt not steal," "Do not be a non-traditional shopper."

• Instead of "Thou shalt not commit adultery," "You shall not be sexually dysfunctional."

Back to the Basics

Do you see why giving God a makeover just won't work? Without the foundations of the faith—trust in Jesus that includes repentance, obedience to God's laws, and respect for the whole of God's Word—Christianity isn't Christianity. It's impossible to take a little off here, and a little off there and come up with the same gospel Jesus preached. Cut-and-paste Christianity is just not possible.

Remember, it is Christ who changes us—not the other way around.

Now for the real issue: could anyone fall away from the faith? Could you? Could I? Could you and I ever become casualties of the end times? The answer is "yes." Regardless of how many souls we have won to Christ, how much Scripture we have memorized, how much time we have devoted to prayer and Bible study, and what we have done in the past to serve Christ, each of us has the potential to fall.

LET'S PRAY

Father, we believe that we are living in the last days. We believe that Jesus will soon come back to earth to establish His kingdom. We see what the devil is doing daily in the world around us. We acknowledge that these are dangerous, uncertain times. We realize that some have already thrown in the towel and abandoned the faith. And we see that temptation is strong. We pray that You will show us how to stand so that we do not become casualties of the end times. Help us, Lord, to recommit ourselves to You. Teach us to serve You with greater intensity. May we be strengthened. May we become bolder. Open our eyes that we may see the snares and pitfalls before us, so we can avoid falling into them. Open our eyes that we may see the areas of compromise we were previously blinded to. Help us, Lord, to receive this message with joy. May this message sink deep into our hearts. In Jesus' name, we pray. Amen.

2

COME ON—THIS IS SERIOUS!

Therefore let him who thinks he stands take heed lest he fall.

—*1 Corinthians 10:12*

Believe it or not, I used to be a junior herpetologist! That's right—I liked snakes. I not only liked snakes, snakes were my hobby. I had lots of them—boas, pythons, king snakes, and gopher snakes. I had snakes in all shapes and sizes. I saved my money to buy more of them. After all, my career goal at that time was to one day open a pet shop specializing in—you guessed it—snakes. This, of course, drove my mom a little nuts. My mom is very happy now that I no longer collect snakes or have any interest in them. My wife, Cathe, is pretty thrilled about that too, come to think of it. But as a kid, I thought snakes were the ultimate.

In the course of pursuing my strange hobby, I met a guy I really admired. To me, he seemed somewhat of a hero. After all, he took the herpetologist thing one step further and collected *venomous* snakes! He worked in some type of zoo and actually had been bitten once by a tiger snake. For those of you who don't know, the tiger snake is one of the deadliest of all venomous snakes. Its bite is far more lethal than that of a cobra. This guy had been bitten by a tiger snake—and survived! As I got to know him, I learned that the reason he survived was because he had been injecting himself for years with tiger snake serum and had finally built up an immunity to it. So when he was bitten by a tiger snake, he was able to survive—barely.

Thereafter this guy apparently thought he was indestructible. No snake would ever take *him* down! He bragged and bragged about how he had survived the bite of the tiger snake. Then he got even bolder. He started letting venomous snakes loose in his house. They would slither over the furniture, creep across the floor, and inch up the walls. By venomous snakes, I mean cobras that had not been defanged—that sort of thing. One day he was bitten by a cobra that he had allowed to slither freely through his house. He didn't even realize it at first. Not until his leg began to swell and ache did he realize that he had been bitten by one of his cold-blooded "friends." He was rushed to the hospital, where he died.

Here was a man who thought that because he had survived the bite of the tiger snake, he didn't have to worry about a few little cobras. Because he became too casual in dealing with the enemy, he eventually reached a point where he refused to take his enemy seriously. He let his guard down, and that became his downfall.

Let's Not Get Too Cozy with the Enemy

There is a lesson Christians can learn from this man's tragic story. There are those who think, "I'm strong. I can handle this. I'll never fall." Perhaps it's true: the big things do not present a problem. But what about the little things? Too often, it's the little things that bring Christians down. Why? Because, like the guy who had been bitten by a tiger snake, they become overconfident. With a few big victories under their belts, they think they can handle anything and everything. They let their guards down, only to be defeated later by some relatively small thing.

It reminds me of a story I heard once about a hunter and a bear. The hunter went deep into the woods to search for bear. It seems he wanted to shoot one and skin it for its coat. After a long wait, the hunter finally had a huge brown bear in his sight. He wrapped his finger slowly around the trigger, holding the barrel steady, aiming for the center of the hulking animal's forehead. But just as he was preparing to squeeze the trigger, the bear turned around and, catching the hunter by surprise, said in a soft voice, " Wait! Let's talk this thing over! Isn't it better to talk than to shoot? What is it you really want? Why don't we negotiate?"

Lowering the shotgun, the hunter replied, "Well, actually, all I want is a fur coat!"

And the bear admitted, "All I want is a meal!"

As the two sat down to negotiate, the hunter dropped his guard and set his gun down on a big grey rock. After a while the bear walked out of the forest alone. Apparently the negotiations were successful. The bear had a full stomach and, in a manner of speaking, the hunter had his fur coat.

Lessons from the Wilderness

Several specific sins listed in 1 Corinthians, chapter 10 caused the Israelites—God's chosen people—to be "overthrown in the wilderness." They include sexual immorality, idolatry, and looking back—living in the past. In the pages of *The Great Compromise*, we will thoroughly examine these potential pitfalls—pitfalls commonly faced today by Christians. As we do, we will see the common thread of compromise clearly emerge; for it is compromise that we are seeking to identify and destroy. Here is what that passage of Scripture says:

> Moreover, brethren, I do not want you to be unaware that all our fathers were under the cloud, all passed through the sea, all were baptized into Moses in the cloud and in the sea, all ate the same spiritual food, and all drank the same spiritual drink. For they drank of that spiritual Rock that followed them, and that Rock was Christ.
>
> But with most of them God was not well pleased, for their bodies were scattered in the wilderness. Now these things became our examples, to the intent that we should not lust after evil things as they also lusted. And do not become idolaters as were some of them. As it is written, *"The people sat down to eat and drink, and rose up to play."* Nor let us commit sexual immorality, as some of them did, and in one day twenty-three thousand fell; nor let us tempt Christ, as some of them also tempted, and were destroyed by serpents; nor murmur, as some of them also murmured, and were destroyed by the destroyer.
>
> Now all these things happened to them as examples, and they were written for our admonition, on whom the ends of the ages have come. Therefore let him who thinks he stands take heed lest he fall. No temptation has overtaken you except such as is common

to man; but God is faithful, who will not allow you to be tempted beyond what you are able, but with the temptation will also make the way of escape, that you may be able to bear it.

—1 Corinthians 10:1–13

Can't you just hear the Israelites talking among themselves? "We'll never fall! We went through the Red Sea together. We were fed by manna. We drank water from the Rock. God took care of us!"

Isn't that just like the Church? "Wait a second—I have received Christ. I have been baptized. I receive communion. I have led people to the Lord. I'll never fall!"

Wait a minute! You are *not* above falling and falling hard. The moment you begin to lower your guard, watch out. This is exactly what Paul warned about in 1 Corinthians, chapter 10.

Consider for a moment who Paul was preaching to in 1 Corinthians, chapter 10. These were the believers at Corinth. The great apostle Paul personally instructed them. But Paul was warning them, "You cannot think that you are incapable of falling into sin. Learn from the example of Israel."

To illustrate this point, Paul used the familiar story of the Jews' exodus from Egypt. We know that the Jewish people had repeatedly cried out for a deliverer from Pharaoh's cruel tyranny. Amazingly enough, God was grooming such a man in Pharaoh's own court. Most of you are familiar with the events surrounding the arrival of the child, Moses, into the court of Pharaoh. Schooled in the ways of Egyptian royalty, he was being groomed for leadership. If he had played his cards right, so to speak, he might have been Egypt's next Pharaoh. But God had something else in mind for Moses.

Right Idea, Wrong Time to Use it

One day Moses saw an Egyptian beating a Jew. In a fit of moral outrage, he killed the Egyptian. Moses had the right idea but went about it in the wrong way. In other words, he knew the Jews needed a deliverer, but instead of waiting on the Lord's timing and instruction, he took things into his own hands and was driven into exile for forty years. But in those forty years, living as a wanted man, God worked in Moses' life and made him into the man He wanted him to be. It has been said that Moses spent forty years in Pharaoh's court, finding out that he was somebody. Then he spent forty years in the desert, finding out that he was nobody. Finally he spent forty years leading the children of Israel through the wilderness, finding out what God can do with a somebody who finds out that he is a nobody. I think you get the picture.

When the time was right, Moses boldly stormed into Pharaoh's court with the demand, "Let My people go!" Pharaoh wasn't exactly responsive to his demands. He required a little proof that Moses actually was speaking for the Most High God. Through a series of miracles, Pharaoh was finally brought around to God's way of thinking.

As if this were not miracle enough, the Jews began to murmur and complain. When they finally reached the borders of the Promised Land, they shrank back in fear and unbelief. They had finally taxed God's patience. After all, He had sent their deliverer. He had vanquished Pharaoh's army. He had parted the Red Sea. He had brought them to the Promised Land. He had even put up with their idolatry, immorality, and constant complaining. What were a few giants to Him?

He sentenced them to wander for forty years in the wilderness, but even that judgment was tempered by God's supernatural provision. He met their needs. Rocks broke open and gushed forth water. Manna fell from heaven to provide pleasant-tasting food that did not require any type of labor other than gathering it each morning. He led them by a cloud of smoke by day and a pillar of fire by night. He sustained them and led them every step of the way through their wilderness journey.

Yet we know that of the approximately two to three million Jews who fled from Egypt, only two of that original group of Israelites made it into the Promised Land. I wouldn't say that was a very good average, would you? Two people out of two to three million. Something really went wrong. For forty years the Israelites wandered in circles in the wilderness until every unbelieving one of them had died. Only two whose faith stood God's test were allowed to enter in.

The Same, Now as Then

It's the same with us. Like Israel, we want change. We want deliverance. One day Jesus awakens in us a sense of need for Him. We cry out to Him, receive Him into our hearts, and begin to follow Him. But, unfortunately, not every one who professes faith in Jesus Christ will finish the course. Some will fall away. Some will begin to follow Him but become sidetracked.

Why did the Israelites start out with a bang, only to end with a whimper? The answer is simple: they wanted to see how far they could "push the envelope." They took His freedom for granted. They tried to live on the edge. Instead of staying close to the God who had led them out of bondage, they took the blessings, provisions, and direction of God for granted. They misused what they had been so freely given, and eventually they lost everything.

Whose fault was it that the Israelites fell in the desert? It is clear that their failure was not due to a lack of provision. At no time did the Israelites accuse God of failing them. No, their failure was a result of compromise. They played around with sin, so sin played around with them.

Sin is a very insidious thing. At first it seems so harmless—then its bite proves fatal. As the evangelist Billy Sunday wisely observed, "One reason that sin flourishes is that it is treated like a cream-puff instead of a rattlesnake."

Here I go with another snake analogy! I once read a newspaper story about a toddler who had found a baby rattlesnake and began playing with it, not realizing that his "toy" was a deadly serpent. The newspaper story pointed out that a single drop of venom from a baby rattler is much more potent than the same amount of venom from a fully grown rattlesnake. This child's mother found the child, happily at play, holding the deadly reptile in his hand like a toy rattle. She also discovered that the rattler had already bitten her child. The child was rushed to the hospital and, fortunately, survived. But the story could have ended tragically, had the mother not found the child before the venom produced its lethal results.

In the same way, some Christians "play" with sin, thinking it won't bite. Maybe it's a sin that seems to be "small"—just a "little one." That single compromise can give a person a false sense of security. After all, nothing happened as a result of just one compromise. But Satan has wedged his foot inside the door. In order for him to gain a foothold in our lives, he will need our assistance. When we compromise—when we allow those "little sins" to mount up—we are giving the devil the assistance he needs to set up a stronghold.

Who Made You Do it?

Sin always costs something. Look at the case of the Israelites. It cost them everything. It still costs everything. That old standby excuse, "The devil made me do it," just doesn't cover it.

Now, you may say, "But the devil *really did* make me do it!" But just wait a minute. I'm not saying the devil didn't play a part, or that his power is not considerable. I am saying that every person is responsible for his or her own spiritual success or failure. What do I base this belief upon? First Corinthians 10:13. This passage of text assures us that God won't give us more than we can handle. Jesus knows our breaking point. He knows how much we can take. When God lets His children go through fiery trials, He always keeps one eye on them and one finger on the thermostat. He knows how much heat we can stand. Remember, He has made a way of escape in the midst of every temptation (see 1 Cor. 10:13). Therefore, if we succumb to the enticements and temptations of the devil, we must take responsibility for that.

Let's go back a little further, to the Garden of Eden. You might say, "Isn't it true that Eve was beguiled by the serpent to eat the forbidden fruit?" I agree—she was beguiled by the serpent. But I maintain that the serpent wouldn't have had the opportunity to beguile her if she hadn't been listening to him. Had she "resisted the devil," the serpent would have had no opportunity to whisper in her ear. Certainly, the devil tempted her. But she was in the wrong place at the wrong time, listening to the wrong voice. As a result, she did the wrong thing. The lesson as applied to Israel is that they made the wrong choices and were ultimately defeated as a result of those choices.

The pitfalls that beset the Israelites are the same ones end-time believers must guard against. Just when we feel the most secure within ourselves, just when we think our spiritual life is at its strongest, just when we're convinced that our doctrine is the soundest, our morals are the purest, and our lives are the most stable, we should be the most dependent on the Lord. We should be vigilant to stand guard during these times of apparent safety, more than at any other time. When we think we've reached some spiritual plateau, we are in the most jeopardy. Then the Spirit of the Lord will come in and begin to gently nudge us, "Warning! You're getting close to the edge! Be careful now!"

When Strength is Really a Weakness

Sometimes the weakest Christian is not in as much danger as the strongest one. You see, our strongest virtues can also be our greatest vulnerabilities.

Consider some of the great personalities of the Bible. They experienced times of vulnerability too. Moses was known as the meekest man on the face of the earth, yet pride and presumption dealt him a fatal blow. Samson, a man of supernatural strength, fell because he yielded to his natural desires. Peter discovered that in the area where he believed himself to be the strongest, he was actually weak. Elijah, known for great bravery and boldness, was paralyzed by fear. Each of these individuals had at least one encounter in which their strengths became their weaknesses.

Paul, speaking to the Corinthians, was not speaking to weak, frail believers. He was addressing those who knew the Lord—those who had privileges, who had backgrounds with Christ. They were capable—even vulnerable to—falling because they had lowered their guard by thinking that they were above it.

We must never rest on our laurels. The mature believer realizes that there is always a long way to go. He or she realizes there is always the potential and propensity for sin within them. Consequently, mature believers are ones who constantly keep their guards up. Consistency is the mark of maturity.

I once heard the story of a young captain who served in the ranks of Napoleon's army. When he was recommended for a military promotion, Napoleon asked, "Why do you suggest this man for promotion?" His commanding officer answered, "Well, out on the battlefield several days ago, he displayed unusual courage and, as a result, a victory was won." "Good," replied Napoleon. "What did he do the next day?" As you may have guessed, the conversation ended right there—and so did this man's dream of promotion.

In much the same way, we can see the insignificance of our claims of what we once did for the Lord. What did we do next? What are we doing today? What do we plan to do tomorrow? We can't live in the past. Our relationship with Christ should be fluid and growing. It requires constant maintenance and cultivation. The day we stop being built up in our most holy faith is the day our faith will begin to start breaking down. Then we will become sitting ducks—far more vulnerable than ever to the enticements and temptations of the devil.

Of course, the best defense is a good offense. The best way not to go backward is to keep going forward. So let's not be satisfied with what we once did for Christ. Let's not live in the past. Let's press forward, take up our crosses daily, and follow Him. Remember, "His mercies are new every morning" (see Lam. 3:23). Let's apply the wisdom of that scripture on a daily basis. As we seek to move forward in Christ, we will not be nearly as vulnerable to the enemy as if we were standing still, "sitting duck" targets to the devil's flaming arrows.

LET'S PRAY

Lord, help us to be watchful, vigilant, to keep our guards up as we walk with You. Keep us from feeling that we are spiritually "indestructible." Help us to walk humbly before You at all times. And help us to move forward, learning and growing as we seek to serve You. In Jesus' name, we pray. Amen.

3

THE DEVIL IS REAL—LITERALLY

Be sober, be vigilant; because your adversary the devil walks about like a roaring lion, seeking whom he may devour.

—*1 Peter 5:8*

I s the devil a real person or merely the sum of everything evil? Many Americans certainly believe in the devil. They're just not sure who—or what—he is. A recent Gallup Poll revealed that as many as 70 percent of Americans believe there is a real devil; it also revealed that only half that number see him as a personal being.

Is the devil personal? If so, I certainly don't want to get very personal with him. But this issue raises some very good questions. Is the devil an actual personality? Or is he just a force? Is he an intelligent being, capable of carrying out complicated strategies with a distinct agenda in mind? Or is the term "devil" simply used to define a random sequence of events connected with evil?

The Origin of Evil

One may well ask, "Where did someone as wicked as the devil originate?" and even, "Why would a loving God create someone as wicked and horrible as Satan?" In fact, I have even wondered why God would not simply allow us to live in an evil-free world, absent of Satan and the stain of sin and suffering. I have come to realize, however, that while such a world would be wonderful, it would also be radically different than ours today. One of the most noticeable restrictions would be the absence of free will. One of humanity's distinguishing features is free will—the ability to choose one's direction in life. God did not create robots. He created human beings and gave each person a free will. Free will is a bit like a double-edged sword—it can be used for good . . . or evil.

God does not wish to receive worship from preprogrammed automatons anymore than we would like to hear "I love you" in the computerized voice of a wind-up doll. It just doesn't seem to have the same heartfelt expression as your own child telling you, "I love you" as you tuck him into bed. There's something extra special about hearing those three little words from someone who chooses to say them because he or she really means it.

It is important to note that God did not create Satan to be wicked. He did not create the devil, or Satan, as he is called in Scripture. His created state was that of Lucifer, whose name means "light." In fact, we are told that his original created state was as a beautiful angelic being—the most beautiful of all the angels. He seemed to have great power and influence in heaven. He was called the "anointed cherub" (Ezek. 28:14). The Bible describes his covering as alight with beautiful, precious stones.

Interestingly enough, the Bible only lists three angels by name—the archangel Michael, the angel Gabriel, and Lucifer, who later became the devil. We are not told exactly how angels are ranked in heaven, but we know that Lucifer ranked high among them. Describing him, Ezekiel 28:15 and 17 state, "You were perfect in your ways from the day you were created, till iniquity was found in you. . . . Your heart was lifted up because of your beauty; you corrupted your wisdom for the sake of your splendor; I cast you to the ground. . . ." A more literal translation of that description would be, "You had the seal of perfection, full of wisdom, perfect in beauty." So from this passage of text, we know that Lucifer was a beautiful angelic being.

Scripture gives us even more insight into this fascinating but completely wicked fallen angel in the Book of Isaiah, which contains this descriptive passage: "How you are fallen from heaven,

O Lucifer, son of the morning! How you are cut down to the ground. . . . For you have said in your heart: 'I will ascend into heaven, I will exalt my throne above the stars of God. . . . I will ascend above the heights of the clouds, I will be like the Most High'" (Isa. 14:12–14). God then gives His answer to this strutting, egocentric being: "Yet you shall be brought down to Sheol, to the lowest depths of the Pit" (Isa. 14:15).

At one time Lucifer dwelt in the presence of God Himself (see Ezek. 28:13). Music was apparently involved with his ministry, for the Bible says music was found in his wings. It is safe to say, then, that Lucifer was in some capacity involved in praise and worship in heaven. But he was not satisfied with worshiping God. He wanted to be worshiped. Because of the intensity of his own greed and ambition, this once-beautiful, very powerful angel lost his position and honor in heaven. He was cast out of heaven, along with one-third of the angels who chose to rise up in rebellion with him. Forever banished to an eternity in the lake of fire, the devil and his angels now had a new agenda. If they could not assume God's throne, and if they could not avoid eternal damnation, then they would at least take as many human souls as possible with them into the eternal lake of fire.

Since his rejection from heaven, the devil has established a very well-defined set of goals. He knows his time is limited, his opportunities short-lived, and his sentence sure. Therefore, in these last days he has dramatically stepped up his efforts to oppose mankind. You might say he has pulled out all the stops, and even that he has gone for the jugular! Why else would we be seeing such a mass abandonment of godly principles, such an increase of "feel good" religions which have no basis in Scripture, and such an increase in exultation of self? Make no mistake about it—the devil knows exactly what his future holds.

The Devil a Believer?

Believe it or not, the devil believes in Jesus Christ. In fact, in one sense, he is very orthodox in his beliefs. If I were ever to sit down and interview the devil—something I would not want to do—I could ask him certain key doctrinal questions. I'd ask things like, "Do you believe in the virgin birth?" and "Do you believe in the inspiration of Scripture?" I might ask him if he believes Jesus was—and is—the Son of God. After all, he affirmed it himself during his forty-day temptation of Jesus in the wilderness when he said, "If you are the Son of God. . . ." (Matt. 4:3). I might even ask him if he believes in the return of Christ to earth. I believe his answer to every one of these questions would be "yes"—but a qualified "yes."

While it is true that the devil believes in the inspiration of Scripture, it is also true that he hates and opposes it. Although it is true that the devil believes in the literal return of Christ to earth, it is also true that until then he is busy creating as much havoc and turmoil on earth as possible. Although it is true that he believes in the virgin birth, it is also true that he actively tried to stop it from happening and has masterminded a plot to discredit the doctrine among Christians. The Bible says, "The demons believe—and tremble!" (James 2:19). So it is true that the devil and his demons believe in the truth of God's Word. But it is also true that they are vehemently, violently opposed to it.

We know that the devil's days on earth are numbered. But the devil knows it too. Therefore, as I have already stated, his objective is to draw as many people as possible down into hell with him. His main plan is to keep people from ever coming to know Christ. After that his plan is to cause those who have accepted Christ to stumble and fall. By the way, that's where this message fits in. If the devil actually cannot cause Christians to fall, then he hopes to at the very least immobilize or neutralize them so they will not make a difference in the world. At the very least, the devil hopes to make it impossible for you and me to snatch any more souls out of his clutches.

As I have already pointed out, the Bible clearly teaches that in these last days we will see an increase of demonic activity. As we look at scriptures describing the time known as the Great Tribulation—that seven-year period of time immediately preceding the return of Christ—we find that demonic activity on earth reaches a fevered pitch. What else but a tremendous outpouring of demonic activity could be responsible for the horrendous, perverse wickedness that is present on earth today? How could man, as wicked as he is, even think of such things as the wickedness we now see everywhere around us? There is little doubt that the devil and his forces have inspired this evil.

Four Things the Devil Doesn't Want You to Know

1. The devil doesn't want you to know that he is dramatically outgunned. As I have already pointed out, the devil lost all his position of honor in heaven when his rebellion against the throne of God failed. The Bible tells us that when that event transpired, he was cast out of heaven and took one-third of the angels along with him. We are not certain how many angels that is. But Scripture tells us there are millions and millions of angels. I believe the angels who followed Lucifer in his rebellion against God are now the demon spirits that are so active in this world. The devil—Satan—is a fallen but still-powerful spirit being. He is commanding a well-organized network of demon powers who share the goal of helping him accomplish his evil purposes on planet earth. What are those purposes? In the words of Christ, those purposes are "to steal, and to kill, and to destroy" (John 10:10).

This demonic army is certainly a force to be reckoned with— and that's the bad news. The good news is that two-thirds of the angels of heaven are *still on our side,* which means *the devil is outnumbered.*

Second Kings, chapter 6, recounts the story of Elisha and his servant who awoke from sleep to discover that the enemy's army was closing in on them. Elisha's servant was first to awaken and spot the invading forces. Frantic, he quickly woke the slumbering prophet: "Oh, my Lord, what shall we do?" To that Elisha replied, "Don't be afraid. Those who are with us are more than those who are with them." Then Elisha prayed, "Lord, open his eyes that he may see." The Lord opened the servant's eyes, and as he lifted them up to the hills, he saw that it was full of angels and horses and chariots of fire. For a brief moment, the stressed out servant was given a glimpse into the supernatural realm—the realm of angels, demons, and God Himself. When he saw that God's angels were already engaged in battle on their behalf, he relaxed. I love that! What an example of trusting God in the midst of trouble! Can you imagine how it would be if God opened your eyes to the supernatural realm so that you could see the angelic armies surrounding you?

God's Word says, "The angel of the Lord encamps all around those who fear Him. . . ." (Ps. 34:7). We are told that the angels are ministering spirits sent forth to minister to those of us who are heirs of salvation (see Heb. 1:13–14). In Psalm 91, we are taught that angels will hold us up and protect us, "lest we dash our foot against a stone" (see v. 12). God's Word assures us that we have angelic protection. In fact, there are more angels on *our side* than on the devil's side.

We must remember that fact when trouble comes our way. Like Elisha and his servant, we must open our eyes and see that we are under God's divine protection. We must remember that the Lord has appointed His angels to protect and keep us.

2. The devil doesn't want you to know that he's been conquered. First John 3:8 states, "For this purpose the Son of God was manifested, that He might destroy the works of the devil." What a powerful Scripture! Colossians 2:14 expands that concept. "He has forgiven you all your sins: Christ has utterly wiped out the damning evidence of broken laws and commandments which always hung over our heads, and has completely annulled it by nailing it over His own head on the cross. And then, having drawn the sting of all the powers ranged against us, he exposed them, shattered, empty and defeated, in his final glorious triumphant act!" (Col. 2:14, PHILLIPS).

Shattered! Empty! Defeated! Did you hear that? Jesus has disarmed the devil and his demon powers. When Jesus proclaimed, "It is finished!"—the battle cry of the cross—those words reverberated throughout heaven and hell. Satan and his demon cohorts had been defeated. Christians today share the victory. This means we need not attempt to contend with this powerful fallen angel using merely our human strength. We're no match for him—that's obvious. On the other hand, he is no match for us if we stay close to Jesus and wage our warfare from our position in Christ.

That does not mean the devil has no power on earth today. What it means is that he no longer has the upper hand, thanks to the cross. When a child of God puts his or her trust in Christ, they come under His divine protection. It stands to reason that if this is the case, one would want to stay as close as possible to the Source of one's protection. Why is it, then, that so many people are caught up in trying to fly as close to the flame as possible? Instead of staying close to God, they stray away, trying to see just how far they can push it and still retain their salvation. They seem to be trying to see how close they can skate to the lake of fire, without getting their clothes singed. This is dangerous thinking that leads to a dangerous practice. Quite frankly, I have never been able to understand it.

Perhaps it is because I know that the closer I stay to the Lord, the safer I am. I know that when I stay close to the Lord, I am not fighting *for* victory: I am fighting *from* it. In other words, I am standing on the finished work of Calvary, relying on the work that Jesus did on the cross to defeat sin and the devil.

Did you know that this involves one of the basic principles of spiritual warfare, as outlined in Ephesians, chapter 6? Before a word is mentioned about putting on the whole armor of God . . . before we are told about the breastplate of righteousness or the sword of the Spirit . . . before we hear a thing about the helmet of salvation, we are told, "Be strong in the Lord and in the power of His might" (v. 10).

What does this tell me? If I am strong in the Lord and in the power of His might, and if I stay as close to Him as possible, I will be safe. But the devil doesn't want me to do that.

I remember the first time someone stronger than me stood up for me. One cool, New Jersey day when I was just a little boy, I went walking down a street near home, shooting off my brand-new cowboy cap pistols. I was having a good time playing gunslinger when two local bullies showed up and demanded that I surrender my cap pistols. When I refused to give them up, they took them from me and walked off, laughing. I was devastated!

I decided that the only thing a young kid could do under the circumstances was run home and enlist the help of an older—and much bigger—brother. I pleaded my case before my brother, who agreed to search for the thieves and retrieve my cap pistols. I went along to help identify the thugs. It was like an old west showdown complete with six-shooters . . . except it was New Jersey not Tombstone, and I wasn't Wyatt Earp. But my brother was bigger than those two thieves. Finally we found them standing on a street corner, firing off *my* prized cap pistols! Now the tables were turned. My big brother was a whole lot bigger than both of them combined. Suddenly it was the thieves who cowered before *me*. The bullies gladly gave back my cap pistols—not because of my personal strength, but because my big brother stood firmly behind me, ready to back me up. I stood in the strength of my big brother that day.

The same is true in spiritual battle. I stand in the strength of Jesus Christ, recognizing what He did for me at the cross. The devil doesn't want me to know that he was conquered at the cross. He doesn't want me to know that I am safe in the arms of the Lord. He wants to lure me away from safety, and in order to do that, he must find a way to lure me away from the Lord.

I am well aware that the devil expends a great deal of energy in his attempt to lure us away from Jesus. So what do we do when we discover him lurking around, trying to start trouble? The Bible tells us, "Submit to God. Resist the devil and he will flee. . . ." (James 4:7). We are also told not to "give place to the devil" (Eph. 4:27). In other words, God has given us His Word. Now it's up to us to appropriate it.

3. The devil doesn't want you to know that his power is limited. The Book of Job records the tale of how the devil was given permission to test Job's devotion to God. In a terrible chain of events, Job lost just about everything. His servants were murdered. His children were killed in a howling wind storm. His goods were stolen, and to make matters worse, Job was stricken with horrible boils which covered his entire body. His friends deserted him. His wife encouraged him to "curse God and die!" (Job 2:9).

We are given unique insight into the supernatural realm in Job, chapter 1: "One day the angels came to present themselves before the Lord, and Satan also came with them. The Lord said to Satan, 'Where have you come from?' Satan answered the Lord, 'From roaming through the earth and going back and forth in it.' Then the Lord said to Satan, 'Have you considered my servant Job? There is no one on earth like him; he is blameless and upright, a man who fears God and shuns evil.' 'Does Job fear you for nothing?' Satan replied. 'Have you not put a hedge around him and his household and everything he has? You have blessed the work of his hands, so that his flocks and herds are spread throughout the land" (vv. 6–10, NIV).

That's exactly right. The devil was correct. God had put a hedge of protection around Job. He has put an identical hedge of protection around us. From this story, we see that although the devil has considerable power, he does have certain limitations—especially in dealing with a child of God. Before the devil can lay a finger on a child of God, he must first receive permission from our very protective Father in heaven. He can't do just anything he wants. He can't always have his way.

In order to prove Job's faithfulness, God allowed the devil to test his servant by removing many of the possible incentives for Job's devotion. Finally, when it was apparent to all that Job loved God, regardless of whether or not he received blessings, the Lord restored his fortunes and even increased them. Job's faith passed the test.

We are given another example of how Satan must receive permission to approach God's children in the New Testament story of Peter. Peter had been loudly proclaiming his unfailing devotion to Christ. Finally Jesus said to Peter, "Satan has been asking for you by name." Or, to put it another way, "Satan has asked excessively that (all of) you be given up to him—out of the power and keeping of God—that he might sift (all of) you like grain" (Luke 22:31, AMP).

I don't know about you, but if Jesus had said something like that to me, I would be shaking in my sandals. It's frightening to think that Satan would actually approach the throne of God and ask for someone *by name*. Satan asked for Peter by name. That's the bad news. The good news is that Jesus had more to say on the subject: "But I have prayed especially for you [Peter] that your [own] faith would not fail. . . ." (v. 32, AMP).

What a wonderful and comforting thought it must have been when Peter remembered that his Lord had prayed for him. Did you know that Jesus does the same for us? Scripture tells us that Jesus Christ lives to make intercession for us (see Heb. 7:25).

Although the Bible tells us that Peter denied Christ three times on the night He was arrested and, as a result, was driven into deep despair, his faith stood the test and he went on to become one of the leaders of the early Church. He took the message of the gospel to the Jews and was even martyred for his steadfast belief in his Master, Jesus Christ.

The devil couldn't just march in and take Simon Peter—first he had to ask permission. God never would have given permission for the devil to test Peter, had there not been some type of need for that pressure to enter his life. You see, God will allow temptation to enter the life of a believer. He will allow testing. He will allow hardship. But as we have already seen, He will never allow the pressure to reach such a crescendo that we can't endure it successfully. At times it may seem that God has given you more than you can handle, but during these times we must trust that God's Word is true. He says He will not give us more than we can handle, and that's what we must believe.

At times we may protest to God that He has given us more than we can bear, but that's not what His Word says. Sometimes God allows the pressure because He wants us to grow spiritually and learn some valuable lessons that we just wouldn't learn by any other means. Scripture reminds us, "When all kinds of trials and temptations crowd into your lives, my brothers, don't resent them as intruders, but welcome them as friends! Realise that they come to test your faith and to produce in you the quality of endurance. But let the process go on until that endurance is fully developed, and you will find you have become men of mature character, with the right sort of independence." (James 1:2–4, PHILLIPS).

4. *The devil doesn't want you to know that he can't be everywhere at once.* That's right—the devil is not omnipresent. Only God is omnipresent, which means He has the ability to be all places at all times with all people. The devil can only be in one place at one time. That's why he relies so heavily on his demons to carry out his evil agenda. When we say, "The devil was tempting me," or "The devil has really been hassling me," we are saying, in effect, that one of the devil's henchmen has been giving us a hard time. I don't know that most of us have actually encountered the devil himself. In effect, we are being confronted by the devil when one of his demons is assigned to create trouble in our lives. But it is usually not the devil doing it—it's just a member of his demonic army.

Dangerous Warnings

Sometimes there are warning signs to tell us that we are in danger of falling. One of them is thinking that it could never happen to us. We are in grave danger when we think or say things like, "I know people who have fallen away from the Lord, abandoned Him, or fallen into some type of sin. But *I* have never done anything like that! *I* have never committed any of those horrible sins!"

In 1 Corinthians 10:12, the apostle Paul warns against thinking we could never give in to a particular temptation: "Let him who thinks he stands take heed lest he fall." Here is a more literal translation: "Therefore, let the man who imagines himself to be standing so securely see to it lest he fall, and he can avoid falling." I really like that part. *You can avoid falling.* That's right—you *can* avoid falling. So be careful. You're in jeopardy when you think falling is something that could never happen to you.

Look what happened in the life of King David. He had served the Lord faithfully for twenty years when he fell into sin with Bathsheba. For twenty years the power of God had come upon him in a profound way. It is often those who have known the Lord the longest who can become the most vulnerable because they start resting on their laurels and don't realize that maintaining their relationship with the Lord takes work.

In essence, therefore, the weakest Christian is not in as much spiritual danger as the one who is strong. The weaker Christian may at least acknowledge his weakness and desire to walk closely with the Lord. The stronger one may think, "It won't happen to me! I'll never fall!" In that case, strength becomes weakness. Virtue becomes vulnerability.

Consider the church at Laodicea. They boasted about their spirituality. God's assessment of the church at Laodicea, however, was a bit different. He said to them, "You say, 'I am rich. I am wealthy. I don't need a thing.' But you don't realize you are wretched, you are pitiful, you are poor, you are blind, and you are naked" (see Rev. 3:17). The Laodiceans thought they were strong, but God saw their "strength" as weakness.

This was essentially Simon Peter's problem. He had just boasted to Jesus, "Though all deny you, I will never deny you" (see Mark 14:29–30). We know how that story ended.

This is why we must be careful not to become like the self-righteous Pharisee who "prayed thus with himself, 'God, I thank You that I am not like other men. . . .'" (Luke 18:11).

What a self-centered way of praying! Then he said, "I thank You that I am not like this tax collector over here." I wonder if he prayed loudly enough so the tax collector standing nearby could hear him? Even if he could have heard him, he probably would not have lifted his face from his prayers. He was busily crying out, "God, be merciful to me a sinner!" (v. 13).

What an arrogant man was this Pharisee. How correct was Scripture in stating, "He prayed thus with himself." God didn't hear that proud man's prayers. Instead, He heard the penitent, honest, heartfelt prayers of the tax collector. He heard the prayers of the man who saw himself as God sees mankind, not the boastful prayers of a man who saw himself as high and lifted up. That is God's position, isn't it?

A Real, Personal Enemy

It has been said, "You can tell a lot about a man by who his enemies are." The same is true in this spiritual battle we are engaged in. Yes, I used the word, "battle." Many believers are shocked to discover that the Christian life is not a playground, but a battleground! The Christian life is far from one of ease. It is a life marked by conflict, spiritual warfare, and intense opposition. We are no longer in opposition to God; our conflict with Him has ended. When we surrendered our lives to Jesus Christ and made Him our Commander-in-Chief, we also acquired a new enemy—a powerful spirit-being with a large network of demon forces at his beck and call. Now that we belong to Jesus, our new enemy— the devil—has set the crosshairs of his sights squarely on us.

Scripture not only likens the Christian life to war—it actually *calls* it war. The choice of whether we win or lose is up to us. We must decide whether we will move backward, forward, or just tread water. But make no mistake—if we choose to move forward in the things of God, there *will* be opposition.

Many years ago someone asked the great evangelist, Charles Finney, "Do you believe in a literal devil?" Finney's response was classic: "You try opposing him for awhile and you'll see if he is literal or not." I'd say that's a pretty good rule of thumb, even today. If you want to discover whether or not there is a literal devil, just start serving Jesus and seeking His will for your life. Soon enough you'll find out just how real the devil is.

The Devil Wears Many Faces

Victor Hugo once said, "A good general must penetrate the brain of his enemy." Because we are engaged in spiritual battle, it helps to know a few things about our adversary's strategies. Although Satan is a brilliant strategist, he is not all that imaginative. Therefore, he must do the same things over and over again. Make no mistake about it: the devil has many clever strategies, plans, and tricks up his sleeve. Yet he moves in predictable patterns, using the same tactics he has used for centuries. Do you think he is operating by that popular adage, "If it ain't broke, don't fix it"? Perhaps he *invented* it.

Satan is sometimes a dangerous wolf, disguised as a sheep. Sometimes he roars like a lion, but more often he comes like a serpent, in all his depravity and horror. And sometimes he comes as an angel of light. Someone once wrote, "You may be resisting him on one hand and setting up house with him on the other!"

Sometimes he comes disguised as a wolf in sheep's clothing. Sometimes he is invisible but exerts a powerful influence, as "prince of the power of the air" (Eph. 2:2). Sometimes he is Satan, coming as a roaring lion. Sometimes he comes as an angel of light, appearing to be full of truth. Sometimes he is just the devil. It helps to know that the devil wears many faces.

One of the personas of the devil is a wily serpent, as depicted in the Genesis account of the serpent who beguiled Eve and brought about the fall of mankind. Since I've had a bit of experience with snakes, I find this particular aspect of the devil quite interesting.

Back to a snake analogy: remember, I had snakes as pets when I was a kid. I kept different varieties of slithering reptiles in several terrariums which I had set up in my room. My collection included boas, king snakes, gopher snakes, ribbon snakes, and others. I learned there's a funny thing about snakes: you never know what they're thinking. They're cold-blooded. They don't have expressive faces like other pets. Dogs, for instance, are very easy to read. You can easily tell when a dog is happy, sad, or angry. But a snake's expression is always the same. A snake may be thinking about biting you, and you would never know it—until it actually happened.

Satan is much the same. He cleverly "snakes" his way into different areas of our lives, seeking to gain a foothold. Ideally, he would like to make it seem that he doesn't even exist. He works hard to promote the lie that "the devil" is merely some fictional character who appears on Saturday morning TV, a short guy dressed in a cute red suit, carrying a pitchfork. To fall for a lie like that is just not biblical. If the devil can't sell you that one, then he'll try to catch you in some type of compromise and thus erode your faith—for as long as it takes to finally bring you down.

We must never underestimate the devil, for if we do, we do so at our own peril! Yet we must at all times be aware that for believers, he is a defeated foe.

LET'S PRAY

Lord, help us to know our enemy and to not be ignorant of his devices. Give us insight into the devil's strategies. Keep us from overestimating his power or position as "the god of this world." But most importantly, keep us from underestimating his position as a defeated foe. Help us to stand fast on the finished work of Calvary, safe in the knowledge that Jesus came to destroy the works of the devil. And He did! Help us to see that You, Lord, are our place of safety. Keep us close, secure in the knowledge of Your protection and love, and safe from the snares of compromise. In Jesus' name, we pray. Amen.

PART 2

THE FACES
OF COMPROMISE

4

LEAD US NOT INTO TEMPTATION

No temptation has overtaken you except such as is common to man; but God is faithful, who will not allow you to be tempted beyond what you are able, but with the temptation will also make the way of escape, that you may be able to bear it.

—*1 Corinthians 10:13*

Are you as amazed by computers as I am? They can seem to be so . . . *human*. They have *memories*. They catch *viruses*. Viruses can be lethal to a computer's hard drive. That's why most computers are now equipped with programs that intermittently check for the pesky invaders, then "inject" them with a program that wipes the critters out before they can do damage to the system or sabotage important files. Computers "catch" viruses in various ways. They can be carried in on defective software. They can be deliberately planted by crafty "hackers" who crash through a computer's security system to wreak intentional havoc. However these viruses are transmitted, they seem to just pop up from nowhere. They can cause a lot of damage, cost a lot of money, even destroy files that are impossible to replace. So anyone who owns a computer wants to be constantly on the alert for these strange viruses. They are *so sneaky!*

Satan, too, is sneaky. But in order to invade our "system," he needs our cooperation.

The Tempter

One of the personas of Satan is the Tempter. It has been my experience that in order for the Tempter to be successful in his evil agenda, he also needs a "temptee." Who is the "temptee?" Anyone who is tempted, of course. How many times have you heard, "The devil made me do it?" For that matter, how many times have you said, "The devil made me do it?" Come on—face it. The devil didn't *make* you do it. He just presented the suggestion to do it. You're the one who *decided* to take him up on it.

The truth hurts, doesn't it? But it also sets you free. However, I have heard someone say that "The truth sets you free, but first it will make you miserable!" Have you ever experienced the misery that comes with conviction? Certainly—we all have. But thank God for it. It is the conviction of the Holy Spirit that leads us to repentance, and it is repentance that brings us into the place of God's will. Thank God for conviction and repentance!

It means that even if we fall, we can be lifted up again. It means that there is hope. It means restoration and a way back into the center of God's will. First Corinthians 10:13 says, "There hath no temptation taken you but such as is common to man: but God is faithful, who will not suffer you to be tempted above that ye are able [to bear]; but will with the temptation also make a way to escape, that ye may be able to bear it" (KJV).

One of the most common ways Christians are undermined in their walks with the Lord is through temptation. Temptation is a powerful weapon the devil uses with great effectiveness to induce failure, hopelessness, even to destroy believers—especially in these last days. Temptation is a reality we all face daily, and if we're going to face it, we must learn to overcome it. We must learn to resist its enticement if we plan to move forward in the Christian life.

Jesus knew temptation to be a powerful satanic force. That's why He made provision for it in teaching His followers to pray: "Lead us not into temptation, but deliver us from evil. . . ." (Matt. 6:13, KJV).

In chapter 3, we examined certain characteristics associated with the devil. Now let's take a look at the devil's role as Tempter. Just like a virus lurks around a computer's hard drive, trying to find a way in to destroy its "memory," so the Tempter lurks around Christians, trying to find a way in to pollute their minds with thousands of clever and potentially destructive suggestions. These "fiery darts," or "flaming missiles" (AMP), as described in

Scripture, are constantly bombarding the minds of believers. The Tempter never takes a day off. He strikes at the oddest times.

You may be in the midst of reading your Bible, when suddenly some ungodly thought swims through your mind. Perhaps you are caught up in praise and worship at church on Sunday morning, when a truly wicked thought pops into your head. Keep in mind—to be tempted is not to sin. Sin is only sin when temptation is received by you, then acted upon. Until the moment you act upon such a tempting thought, you have a choice. You can recognize the author of such thoughts and choose to reject them—or, as the Bible says, "cast them down"—or you can entertain them, embrace them, and finally act them out.

Why does the enemy place so much emphasis on attacking the minds of Christians? Because the mind is "command central." It is our "computer." It's in charge of our thought life as well as our bodies. In fact, all of our activities are organized and carried out by our brains.

The brain sends tiny impulses to every artery and organ. It regulates our breathing. It determines creativity. It tells every one of our muscles—voluntary and involuntary—to go into action. It tells our eyes when to twitch or blink or even when to cry. It is the seat of dreams and visions. It is where we reason, contemplate, and meditate upon God's Word. It is where our feelings and our attitudes develop, where we make those critical choices that effect our futures—even where we will spend eternity.

The mind is a powerful tool that can reach into the past through our stored up memories and stretch into the future through something called imagination. Why wouldn't Satan go after the mind?

The devil knows that if he can get our minds to dwell on certain sins, then it will be just a matter of time before those sins are acted out. That's why Scripture tells us, "For the weapons of our warfare are not carnal but mighty in God for pulling down strongholds, casting down arguments and every high thing that exalts itself against the knowledge of God, bringing every thought into captivity to the obedience of Christ" (2 Cor. 10:4–5).

We can't stop Satan from knocking at the doors to our minds or from injecting our imaginations with sinful thoughts, but we don't have to let him in.

When someone you don't want to talk to comes to your door, what do you usually do? Have someone else answer the door! Likewise, next time one of these "fiery darts" comes knocking at the door of your mind, have someone else answer. Say, "Jesus, would You mind getting that?" Then see how long those fiery darts linger.

The World, the Flesh, and the Devil

For Satan to accomplish his agenda in the lives of Christians, he needs two things: *the world* and *the flesh*. Perhaps this is why the three terms—the world, the flesh, and the devil—are so often found linked together. The terms "the world" and "the flesh" are also often loosely tossed around in church circles. I hear these terms thrown around so often that I feel they need to be clearly defined, if we are to achieve our goal of learning how to identify and stamp out *compromise*.

When I first became a believer and began to spend time with other Christians, I found their lingo rather mystifying. In an almost cryptic manner, they would say things like, "Brother, that's of *the flesh*" and "That's *worldly!*" Sometimes I would hear someone say, "You shouldn't do that anymore! You're part of *the body* now!" Wait a second—what does that mean? Does it mean that I shouldn't be of *the flesh* because I am finally part of *the body*? I found such "Christianese" confusing. What did statements like, "That person is just too worldly," really mean? Were my fellow believers suggesting that we should no longer live on this earth?

What do terms like "love of this world" and "worldly" really mean? "That's *worldly!*" "Hey, don't *love the world!*" Do statements like these mean that I can't admire a beautiful sunset or a great set of waves and say, "Look what the Lord did?" No, it doesn't mean that at all. I believe Christians can experience a greater appreciation for the beauty of this planet than anyone else on earth. In fact, the Bible even tells us He has richly given us all things to enjoy. To be *worldly* or to *love this world,* however, implies loving this world's system. It speaks of a particular mentality.

While we, as Christians, are free to experience, appreciate, and enjoy nature, we should at the same time keep this appreciation within the proper perspective. We should never *worship* the planet. We should be its stewards. We are not expected to *worship* the environment. We know the earth is important, but we also know that there is something even more important than this earth. The Bible tells us that heaven and earth will one day pass away, but God's Word will never pass away (see Mark 13:31).

How unfortunate it is that there are those today who have decided to worship "Mother Earth." In a very real sense, their religion is environmentalism. Some people today are more excited about *recycling* than they are about *regeneration*. I appreciate God's world, but not at the expense of ignoring those things that will last for all eternity.

Actually, the terms *the world* and *the flesh* are biblical terms—important ones that we should all understand. It is important to note that when the Bible speaks of *the world*, it is not so much concerning this earth we live on, but the world's system—a way of thinking and living that is totally opposed to God. Scripture warns, "Do not love the world or the things in the world. If anyone loves the world, the love of the Father is not in him" (1 John 2:15). James 4:4 enforces that principle: "Whoever therefore wants to be a friend of the world makes himself an enemy of God." In Romans 12:2, the apostle Paul tells us, "Do not be conformed to this world," or as the J.B. Phillips translation puts it, "Don't let the world around you squeeze you into its own mould. . . ."

Why is this world's system so hostile to God? Because of who controls it. The Bible refers to the devil as the "god of this world" (2 Cor. 4:4, KJV). We are warned repeatedly in Scripture against its dangers and allure. Satan's world system is one that is primarily interested in self, giving God no place and no honor. This system fits in nicely with *the flesh,* which always wants to be built up, gratified, petted, and self-exalted. The world appeals to the appetites of the flesh, and mankind's sinful nature and its "me first" mentality. The world and the flesh cooperate to produce the frame of mind that makes one desire to live primarily for self-fulfillment and self-satisfaction, regardless of how one's actions affect others. "Look out for number one"—that's the motto of the world and the flesh. The Bible, however, simply calls it *selfishness*.

First John 2:16 is the classic definition of this phenomenon: "For all that is in the world—the lust of the flesh, the lust of the eyes, and the pride of life—is not of the Father but is of the world."

Now let's apply that to temptation. When you examine temptation, you will usually see that it came in on the heels of one of those three things: the lust of the flesh, the lust of the eyes, or the pride of life. If you look closely at Scripture, you will be able to see Satan's tracks all the way back to the Garden of Eden, because he has been effectively using these three weapons to wage an attack against mankind from the very beginning.

The Lust of the Eyes

When Satan first captivated Eve in the Garden of Eden, he tempted her with the lust of the eyes. Eve *saw* the tree, then she *saw* the fruit of the tree. She fixed her eyes on the forbidden tree, examined the forbidden fruit up close, and began to long for it. "[She] saw that the tree was good for *food*, that it was pleasant to the eyes. . . ." (Gen. 3:6).

Have you ever been on a diet, and gone to a restaurant where a nice, big, juicy pie on display was the first thing you saw when you walked in the door? Have you ever been flipping through the channels of your TV and come across a sexually suggestive music video you were tempted to watch all the way through? Then I don't need to say any more, do I? If you have experienced either of these scenarios, you are quite familiar with this thing known as *the lust of the eyes*. It targets your fantasy and thought life, and when it hits you at a vulnerable moment, it is often very easy to translate those "fantasies" into realities.

The Lust of the Flesh

Satan hit Eve with a "double whammy" back there in the garden. Not only did he tempt her with *the lust of the eyes*, but he also tempted her with *the lust of the flesh*. Having *seen* that the tree was good for food, "she took of its fruit and ate. . . ." (Gen. 3:6). As I pointed out earlier, the flesh primarily speaks of the gratification of our desires. The lust—or desire—of the flesh is the temptation to let one of our God-given drives go out of control. These are our natural drives—appetite, sex drive, attachment to possessions—any physical drive. When one or more of these drives gets out of control, it's time to put the brakes on. These natural, God-given drives can become sinful if taken to extremes and allowed to dominate our lives.

The Pride of Life

This type of temptation is a bit trickier to identify. This clever strategy can take on the form of the pursuit of knowledge (and even morality). It can masquerade as the drive to better oneself. The person who falls prey to this temptation may actually appear to be quite righteous. He may look at others who have fallen to the sins of the lust of the eyes or the lust of the flesh and say, "Thank God, I'm not doing *that!* Thank God, I would never stoop that low. That God, I would never commit such a horrible, depraved sin!" Before you know it, this person has begun to sound just like that self-righteous Pharisee described in chapter 2.

The Pharisee who prayed such ebullient prayers had fallen victim to the pride of life. This type of temptation creeps up on people who begin to think they have all the answers. It can be the root of many other sins. Satan himself was the first personality to commit the sin of the pride of life. He wanted to be like God. Then he wanted to be worshiped instead of God. Look how quickly his spiritual condition deteriorated after that. Beware! This subtle temptation can be one of the worst offenders. Watch out for it.

How Temptation Works

As I have already stated, the devil does the same things over and over again. Identifying a pattern will help us better understand the devil's strategies, because essentially he is doing the very same things on earth today. As you will see, some of these temptations are incredibly obvious and easy to spot. Others, however, are trickier to detect. Easy to spot or hard to detect, why is it that believers seem to fall into the devil's snares anyway? Perhaps it will be helpful to take another peek back at the moment when Eve bit into that expensive piece of fruit. When we do that, we begin to see a pattern developing. What did the devil do in the Garden that he is still doing today? In his excellent book, *The Strategy of Satan,* Warren Weirsbe gives a great outline of Satan's tactics in the Garden.[1]

1. He undermined God's Word. What were those strange thoughts running through the mind of innocent Eve? God had warned Adam and Eve not to eat the fruit from the tree of the knowledge of good and evil. She was well aware of the prohibition. Satan was sly. He was also aware of it. So what did he do? He began to undermine God's Word. Through a series of subtle questions, he caused Eve to question what God had really said about the attractive tree and its beautiful fruit. "Has God indeed said, 'You shall not eat of *every* tree of the garden?" (Gen. 3:1).

Notice that he did not deny that God had spoken. He simply questioned whether God had really said what Eve thought He said. In effect, he was questioning God's love for Eve. He was implying that if God really loved her, He would let her eat from all the trees of the Garden. Because He was not allowing her to eat from this tree, the devil implied that He must be holding something back—something that was good.

Incidentally, this was the same tactic the devil used on Jesus in the wilderness. He said, "If you are God's *beloved* Son, why are you hungry? If you are really God's Son, why has He allowed you to go without food?" (see Matt. 4:3).

And he does the same thing with us today. Given the opportunity, he will question God's love for us. He will whisper, "God doesn't love you! He loves other people, but you aren't worthy of His love. God doesn't really care about you." See how he distorts the truth?

Alfred Lord Tennyson wrote:

"A lie that is all of a lie can be met with and fought outright.
But a lie that is partly the truth is a harder matter to fight."[2]

Remember, Satan—brilliant strategist that he is—won't always question God's Word altogether; rather, he will question what you *thought* He said.

2. He mixed enough truth with the lies so the lies were difficult to detect. By the time the devil had finished filling Eve with his lies, she was really confused. *If the tree's fruit was good to eat, why had God withheld it from her? If it would make her wise, would that not be even better?* By the time such thoughts had taken root, weakening her resolve, the next step was easy. While the devil looked on slyly, she picked some fruit and ate it. Then, when Adam came along, she gave some to him, told him the same thing she had been told—that it was good to eat—and he ate too.

Essentially, the devil told the truth, but he had told a distorted version of it. Eve bought it hook, line, and sinker, however. She bought into the Tempter's pack of lies. And believers are still buying it.

Why is that, when the Bible says we have been given weapons to use against the Tempter?

The Greatest Weapon Against Temptation

So what was Eve going to do? Should she believe the Word of God or the word of the devil? We know how the story ends, unfortunately. How sad that she chose to believe the "father of lies," rather than her Father in heaven, whose infallible Word would have been all it took to defeat her slithery foe.

Eve was not the only one who failed to take up the sword of the Spirit against the enemy back there in the Garden of Eden. Adam also dropped the ball. Each failed to use the most powerful weapon God gave us—and the best one to use when fighting temptation. That weapon is the sword of the Spirit—the Word of God.

In Ephesians, chapter 6, we find a list of the various pieces of spiritual armor that believers are to "wear." These pieces of armor provide powerful protection against the enemy's devices. Isn't it interesting that each one of these pieces is primarily *defensive* in nature, with the exception of the *sword of the Spirit*? It is with the sword of the Spirit that we take offensive position against the enemy, driving him away as Jesus did in the wilderness when he countered each of Satan's accusations with, "It is written. . . . It is written. . . . It is written!" Because the Word was within Him, He was able to draw it out from memory and use it effectively against the devil.

In the same way, when the devil comes and begins to tempt us and challenge us to believe anything except the infallibility of God's Word, we must respond with, "It is written. . . . It is written. . . . It is written!"

The only way we will be able to do that, however, is by committing ourselves to the study and memorization of God's Word.

In order to get it *out of our mouths* in times of trouble, we must first get it *into our hearts and minds*. I cannot stress strongly enough how vitally important it is to become intimately familiar with the Word of God. If you as a believer do not have a working knowledge of Scripture, you will likely become a casualty in this spiritual battle we are in. The devil doesn't care if you read *People* magazine. He doesn't care if you see all the latest movies. (In fact, I'm sure there are some he'd love you to see!) He doesn't necessarily care if you always have your nose planted in the pages of the latest novel—even the latest Christian novel. But he cares if you read the Word of God. Only the Word of God properly used can do him serious damage. The minute you crack open a copy of the Bible, you'd better believe the devil is going to get cranky. He will do his best to distract you with everything he has. Why? Because it's a threat. Only the Word of God will put him to flight.

As you may know, I have the privilege of conducting evangelistic crusades throughout the United States and in several other parts of the world. I meet a lot of people, of course, due to the extensive travel involved with my ministry. Occasionally I meet people who ask me to sign their Bibles. I don't really like to do that because I certainly had nothing to do with writing it. But if they persist, I will usually write something like this: *Sin will keep you from this book, and this book will keep you from sin.*

That just about covers it, doesn't it? *We need to know the Bible.* It's great to carry one around in a briefcase or purse, but it's better to carry it in our hearts. It's great to have one on the shelf, but it's better to know what it contains. It's good to recognize a familiar Scripture passage now and then when we hear it preached, but it's better to be able to quote Scripture passages from memory in the course of prayer. We must study. In Deuteronomy, chapter 11, God instructs us to lay up His words in our hearts, then to teach them to our children, and finally to write them down.

I don't know about you, but I have found that it's easier for me to remember things if I write them down first. I may never have to refer to my notes again, but at least I have them. There is something about writing down information. It seems to ingrain it into my memory. Then when the devil strikes, I've got the ammunition all stored up and ready for him: "It is written. . . ."

Let's return to my "computer" analogy for a moment. I write my books on my computer at home. Occasionally, when I am working on a project on my home computer, a message will flash across the screen: NOT ENOUGH MEMORY! The purpose of the message is to alert me that my hard drive is full. If I plan to continue, I will need to transfer some old files off the hard drive and onto floppy disks to make more room. It means that because the hard drive is full, it will accept no more files. When our "hard drive" is full of the Word of God, the devil can find no place. There is just no room for him to "store" his wicked files. There will be no room because there is NOT ENOUGH MEMORY!

Remember, the best defense to warding off the attacks of the Tempter is a good offense. And there is just no better offense against the enemy known as "temptation" than the proper knowledge and use of the Word of God.

Our Merciful God

"But," you say, "that doesn't apply to me. It's no use; I don't need a good offense because I've already fallen into temptation."

There is still good news for you. Our God is merciful, and His Word contains many promises of restoration to those who have fallen, repented, and come back to Him. After Paul warned believers that everyone has the potential to fall, he added this passage of text: "No temptation has seized you except what is common to man. And God is faithful; he will not let you be tempted beyond what you can bear. But when you are tempted, he will also provide a way out so that you can stand up under it" (1 Cor. 10:13, NIV).

This passage clearly states that God will not allow us to be tempted above our capacity to resist. Temptation in the life of a Christian will always be graded to the fiber of our lives. While we must not overestimate it, thinking we are powerless to resist its pull, we must guard against underestimating it, believing we can handle anything and everything with spiritual effectiveness.

Let me be more explicit: while on the one hand, it is dangerous to believe we'll never fall, on the other hand it is dangerous to believe that we can't help it! Have you ever been there? Believing you are helpless, powerless, unable to stop falling into temptation? You pray and pray for God to deliver you, but you just keep falling.

What makes resisting temptation so difficult for people on this side of the "temptation" spectrum is that they never quite discourage temptation. They seem to pray against temptation, then rush right into places where they secretly know they are most vulnerable. It's the same as putting one's fingers into the flickering flames of a fire, then quickly praying that those fingers won't get burned.

For temptation to "hook" us, we must first listen to it, and—most importantly—desire what it has to offer. James wrote, "Let no one say when he is tempted, 'I am tempted by God' [or 'It's God's fault']; for God cannot be tempted by evil, nor does He himself tempt anyone. But each one is tempted when he is drawn away by his own desires and enticed" (James 1:13–14).

Along these same lines, Paul tells us in the Book of Romans, "Don't you know that when you offer yourselves to someone to obey him as slaves, you are slaves to the one whom you obey—whether you are slaves to sin, which leads to death, or to obedience, which leads to righteousness? But thanks be to God that, though you used to be slaves to sin, you wholeheartedly obeyed the form of teaching to which you were entrusted. You have been set free from sin and have become slaves to righteousness" (Rom. 6:16–18, NIV).

Isn't it true that we sometimes blame God for our stumbling into sin? Somehow, we secretly feel that He is to blame for our spiritual failure. Of course, this is nothing new. Adam did the same thing in the Garden of Eden. After he had eaten the forbidden fruit and was caught red-handed by the Lord, he turned the blame on God in the first known account of "passing the buck": *It's the woman You gave me!* I wonder where Adam placed the emphasis when he made that statement: was it on the word "woman," or was it on the word "You," implying that it was all God's fault?

People today are very prone to buck-passing. We want to blame everyone else for our shortcomings. We call ourselves "dysfunctional." We all have "diseases." Those who are trapped in the homosexual lifestyle say, "It's genetic. I can't help it. I was born this way. I had no choice." Those who are addicted to alcohol say, "I'm not responsible for my actions. It's a disease. I had no choice." When marriages unravel, leaving children desolate and causing great damage to the fabric of our nation as a whole, some people casually explain it away with something like, "We were just incompatible. The love just left our marriage. It was a case of irreconcilable differences!" And when people fall into the snare of adultery, they say, "I couldn't help it. I didn't want to do it. I just got carried away!" I use these illustrations to make the point that it is vital that we take personal responsibility for our decisions and actions in these last days when no one else seems to be willing to do it.

Temptation can and must be resisted. It can be overcome. And when you overcome temptation, there is great blessing. James 1:12 says, "Blessed [or happy] is the man who endures temptation; for when he has been proved, he will receive the crown of life which the Lord has promised to those who love Him." While it isn't easy to resist temptation's pull—especially when you can see that so many of those around you are giving into it daily—it's good to know that there is a great blessing waiting for you when you finally overcome. What a great blessing it is to know that you have passed the test!

A. B. Simpson wrote, "Temptation exercises our faith and teaches us to pray. It is like a military drill and a taste of battle for the young soldier. It puts us under fire and compels us to exercise our weapons and prove their potency. It shows us the recourse of Christ and preciousness of the promises of God. Every victory gives us new confidence in our victorious leader and new courage for the next onslaught of the foe." [3]

So, considering that God will not allow us to be tempted above our capacity to resist, and considering that he will grade each temptation according to the fiber of our lives, we can see that God may even use temptation in our lives to bring about something good. Temptation will cause believers to cling more closely to the Lord. Instead of relying on our own abilities and strengths, it causes us to rely on His. Martin Luther once said, "One Christian who has been tempted is worth a thousand who haven't."

Why Not Turn the Page on Temptation?

When you fall in love with Christ—when He is the passion of your life—this world and all of its temptations and allure just won't hold a candle to Him any longer. All those things that once mattered so much just seem to fade into the distance. I like the words to a song we have sung at Harvest Christian Fellowship for many years: "Turn your eyes upon Jesus, look full in His wonderful face, and the things of earth will grow strangely dim in the light of His glory and grace."[4] Isn't it true? As you fix your eyes upon Jesus, all that junk that once seemed so important just seems to fall away.

It doesn't mean you will no longer be tempted. It doesn't mean you will no longer find yourself vulnerable. It just means you won't want those things more than you want to walk with Jesus—you'll want Him more than anything. Consequently, the world no longer has the appeal it once had. Fall in love with Jesus! That's what I encourage you to do.

I could say, "Stop doing this! Stop doing that! You shouldn't watch this! You shouldn't listen to that!" I could lay down a hundred different rules and regulations. But I know by experience that rules and regulations alone won't help anyone permanently change their behavior. What does work? Simply growing in love for Jesus Christ. That works.

Have you been overtaken by temptation in a certain area of your life? Do you feel like a failure? Like a loser? Now is a great time to do something about it. Why not turn the page? Why not make a fresh start? Choose today to make the break from sin and ask God's forgiveness. By repenting of it and turning from your sin, you are turning your back on failure and turning your face to God, trusting Him to help you resist temptation and defeat it in your life. The Lord is waiting, ready, and willing to go through those fiery trials and temptations with you in the days to come. In fact, He will even carry you through the really tough ones. Why not trust Him today to make you an overcomer?

LET'S PRAY

If you have fallen into temptation and would like to come back to the Lord, why not pray a prayer like this one? God is faithful and will help you overcome the strategies of the Tempter. He will faithfully receive you back into His arms and will restore you.

Father, I have fallen into temptation. I feel like a failure, like a spiritual loser. I ask You to forgive me as I repent of the sin that has overtaken me, and I ask that You deliver me from its snare. As I turn from sin, I turn toward You. Help me to start all over again. Help me to put You first in my life, to study Your Word, and to learn to use it effectively against the enemy, Satan. Father, I pray for a fresh start, for direction in my life. I ask that You bring about something good from this temptation. In Jesus' name, I pray. Amen.

5

WHAT'S YOUR GOLDEN CALF?

You shall have no other gods before Me.

—*Deuteronomy 5:7*

Remember the day you drove your first brand-new car off the showroom floor? The first thing you did was tool around town in it. That's how you used up your first tank of gas. Were you showing off? Well, maybe just a little. . . . You put the convertible top down, took off fast at every light, and turned the stereo up high—the extra-special stereo with special speakers and a CD player that added several hundred dollars to the sticker price. Okay, maybe you were showing off a lot. Why not? You felt like a million bucks. For that matter, you *looked* like a million bucks.

Yes, you looked fantastic in your brand-new car with the top down and your hair blowing gently in the wind—so good, in fact, that you kept glancing in the rearview mirror to see if the other motorists out for a drive that day had the good taste to notice that *your* new car was the best-looking one on the road. You took frequent peeks to see if any heads were turning in admiration of your sleek, custom paint job, sport-pack extras, and tricked-out wheels.

By day two, however, you had become a little paranoid. "Did I remember to lock it? Did I turn on the alarm system? What if someone sideswipes me? What if someone's door bangs into mine after I park? Well, in that case, I'd better park across one-and-a-half spaces. What if—horror of horrors—someone 'keys' my paint job out of a fit of jealous rage? (After all, my car *is* beautiful!) What if that rain storm predicted for this afternoon packs a lot of hail with it? What if. . . ?"

You know the scenario. Before you've run through the long list of things that *might* happen, you realize you've gotten a little crazy over your new car. You acknowledge that this "new car thing" has gotten way out of hand. Instead of you owning *it*, it's more like *it* owns *you*. You wear its emblem emblazoned on your shirt and cap. When people ask to see a photo of your family, you show them the one of your car first—then the photo of your wife and kids. You install one of those new hi-tech alarm systems that detects movement around your car, blaring out a verbal warning: "Step back from this car or you'll be shot!" By now, you have named your car. You speak affectionately to it often, calling it things like "Babe" and "Honey." You admit to yourself that you've lost your perspective where your new car is concerned. You take a moral inventory and finally accept that it's time to get a grip.

Unfortunately, some people never do. That's right—some people never get a grip. Instead of owning their possessions, their possessions own them. There is a term for this condition. It's called *idolatry*.

Idolatry is anything that causes one to bow down in worship. It involves anything we place in a primary position in our lives— that place reserved just for God. After all, does He not command, "Thou shalt have no other gods before Me?" Yet from the very beginning of time, mankind has consistently fashioned little gods for himself and persisted in their worship. It's what the Israelites did, once Moses was safely out of range. While the great deliverer was up on the mountain, receiving God's commandments to His people, they were holding one big bash down below.

The Bible warns us that idolatry will clearly be a temptation and a snare for believers living in the last days. First Corinthians 10:7 tell us, "Do not become idolaters as were some of them (the Israelites)."

With their leader conveniently gone, the Israelites quickly rose up to confront Aaron, who'd been left in charge, with their demands. In Exodus, chapter 32, we read:

Now when the people saw that Moses delayed coming down from the mountain, the people gathered together to Aaron, and said to him, "Come, make us gods that shall go before us; for as for this Moses, the man who brought us up out of the land of Egypt, we do not know what has become of him." And Aaron said to them, "Break off the golden earrings which are in the ears of your wives, your sons, and your daughters, and bring them to me." So all the people broke off the golden earrings which were in their ears, and brought them to Aaron. And he received the gold from their hand, and he fashioned it with an engraving tool, and made a molded calf. Then they said, "This is your god, O Israel, that brought you out of the land of Egypt!" So when Aaron saw it, he built an altar before it. And Aaron made a proc- lamation and said, "Tomorrow is a feast to the Lord." Then they rose early on the next day, offered burnt offerings, and brought peace offerings; and the people sat down to eat and drink, and rose up to play.

And Moses turned and went down from the mountain, and the two tablets of the Testimony were in his hand. The tablets were written on both sides; on the one side and on the other they were written. Now the tablets were the work of God, and the writing was the writing of God engraved on the tablets. And when Joshua heard the noise of the people as they shouted, he said to Moses, "There is a noise of war in the camp." But he said: "It is not the voice of those who shout in victory, nor is it the voice of those why cry out in defeat, but the voice of those who sing I hear."

So it was, as soon as he came near the camp, that he saw the calf and the dancing. [The Israelites were, in fact, engaged in some type of wild sexual orgy, all in the name of "worship," of course.] So Moses' anger became hot, and he cast the tablets out of his hands and broke them at the foot of the mountain. Then he took the calf which they had made, burned it in the fire, and ground it to powder; and he scattered it on the wa- ter and made the children of Israel drink it. And Moses said to Aaron, "What did this people do to you that you have brought so great a sin upon them?" So Aaron said, "Do not let the an- ger of my lord become hot. You know the people, that they are set on evil. For they said to me, 'Make us gods that shall go be- fore us; as for this Moses, the man who brought us out of the land of Egypt, we do not know what has become of him.' And I said to them, 'Whoever has any gold, let them break it off.' So they gave it to me, and I cast it into the fire, and this calf came out'" (vv.1–6, 15–24).

Did you hear that? "Moses, I don't know what went wrong: I just threw some gold in the fire, and *out came this gold calf!*" Give me a break! Here was the man who was second in command over thousands of Israelites reduced to making lame excuses for helping them commit idolatry. Unfortunately, he didn't have a leg to stand on. When we commit idolatry today, we don't have a leg to stand on either.

Please understand, idolatry is not limited simply to the worship of images. It is terrifying but true that a person can faithfully attend church every Sunday and still be caught up in full-tilt idolatry. It's sad but true that some people think that if they go to church on Sundays and observe the various religious rituals, they can do as they wish for the rest of the week, now that they have racked up their quota of "brownie points" with God. I believe, however, that it's better to be a "garden variety" sinner, than an insincere saint. God says of this type of individual, "[They] come near to me with their mouth and honor me with their lips, but their hearts are far from me" (Isa. 29:13, NIV). What makes this particular type of idolatry so terrifying is that God will not tolerate it. He even listed it among His "top ten" sins: "You shall have no other gods before Me. You shall not make for yourself any carved image, or any likeness of anything that is in heaven above, or that is in the earth beneath . . ." (Ex. 20:3–4).

Jesus echoed this message when a lawyer asked Him how he could hope to inherit eternal life. Jesus told him, "You shall love the Lord your God with all your heart, with all your soul, and with all your mind. This is the first and greatest commandment" (Matt. 22:37–38).

Essentially, Jesus was saying that when a person loves God with all his heart, soul, and mind, he will be satisfied. There will be no need to go searching for "things" to fill the void that only God can fill. There will be no need to place another relationship in the position that only God can occupy. I might also add that anyone who is not cultivating a close, intimate relationship with God is in serious jeopardy of stumbling in this area. If that person does not place God first, then it will be just a matter of time before someone—or something—takes His place. With that in mind, let's take a look at some of the potential idols that can crowd God out.

A Few Modern Idols

An idol is anything that takes the place of God in our lives. It is any object, idea, philosophy, habit, leader, occupation, sport, or pastime that is the focus of our primary concern. It is what has first place in our hearts. It is where our loyalty lies. It is whatever decreases our loyalty to God. Alan Redpath defined idolatry this way: "Our god is the person we think is the most precious. For whom we would make the most sacrifice. Who moves our hearts with the warmest love. He (or it) is the person who if we lost him would leave us desolate."[1]

What's your golden calf? Do you have one? Here—let me help you as you take a quick inventory. Is there anything in your life that you are absolutely wild about? Anything you can't live without? Anything you love? Treasure?

Idols can be lots of things. Let's list a few things that qualify as idols.

1. *Other people.* While the Israelites' second idol took the form of a golden calf, their first idol—believe it or not—was Moses. To the Israelites, their godly leader—a man known for his upright lifestyle and personal integrity—was an icon. By his godly and uncompromising lifestyle he was able, apparently, to single-handedly keep two to three million people from turning to idolatry. But the minute he was out of the picture, they flocked to it.

The minute Moses went up to the mountain, the Israelites started looking for a loophole. Essentially, what they were saying was: "Look, Moses was a great guy, and we really respect him as a man of integrity and godliness. But he's just a little too spiritual for us. We can't live that way. In fact, we don't *want* to live that way. What we need is an easy religion that will fit our lifestyle. We've decided to lower our standards a bit. We need a god we can touch—one who appeals to the senses."

There are many people today who are able to stand strong when they're around other Christians. But when you get them off by themselves, they quickly blend into the woodwork. They begin to lower their standards. And before you know it, they've fallen victim to compromise. Aaron was put to such a test, and he failed miserably. Had he been able to stand strong for the Lord, he might have turned the people back from their idolatry. Instead, he helped turn them toward it.

Sometimes people become idols. Perhaps there is a man or woman God used in your life when you were a young Christian. Perhaps this person was instrumental in leading you to Christ, or was a powerful influence for godliness at some point in your walk with the Lord. Perhaps it was a pastor or another leader—someone you greatly admired. Then one day you discovered this person had fallen into sin. Of course, you were greatly shocked—even hurt. Your idol, it seems, had feet of clay after all. They sinned. They fell. They did something you thought they would never do. That's when you said, "That's it—forget this Christianity thing. It's not for me. I'm throwing in the towel. I'm not going to follow the Lord any more."

Wait a minute! Who were you following—God, or the person who disappointed you? Had they taken the place of God in your life? There is a very subtle distinction between admiration and respect for a leader and an unhealthy, idolatrous attachment.

I'm not saying God won't use people to impact our lives and even to influence us in a certain direction. But it's a fact that people are just human, and every person we meet will eventually let us down or fail in some way to measure up to our expectations. Why do we place such unrealistic expectations on others, when they are only human—just like us? I think it's because we want to make idols out of them on a very subconscious level. Then, when they come crashing down from that pedestal we put them on, our faith is shattered. Why? Because it was built upon the wrong foundation. The only reliable foundation is, was, and will always be Jesus Christ.

2. *Possessions.* That's an easier one to spot. A good example from the Bible to illustrate this type of idolatry is the familiar story of the rich young ruler—the young man who went away sorrowfully because Jesus had told him to sell all his possessions, give the money to the poor, and follow Him. He couldn't—or more appropriately, *wouldn't*—do it. Why? Because those possessions had begun to possess him. They were the rich young ruler's idols. It is worth noting that Jesus did not deal

in every person's case the way he dealt with this young rich man. It is apparent that some of His followers were better off financially than others. Why didn't Jesus tell everyone to sell all they had? Because He had looked into this young man's heart and seen the possessions secretly enthroned there. Jesus knew that if this young man were ever to follow Him, he must first give up his idols.

So, in effect, Jesus said to this young man: "Here are My specific, custom-fit directions to you. Gather up everything you have. Sell it. Give the money to the poor. Then follow Me."

But Scripture states that the young man "went away sorrowful" (Matt. 19:22). He would not comply. He just couldn't do it because all the things he owned were more important to him than his relationship with God.

Matthew 6:24 states that "no man can serve two masters: for either he will hate the one, and love the other; or else he will hold to the one, and despise the other. Ye cannot serve God and mammon [money]" (KJV). The Bible also tells us that excessive covetousness is a form of idolatry. By that, I mean, to eagerly desire something that belongs to someone else—to set your heart on something that another person owns. Another way to describe covetousness is to "pant after" something. We see a picture of an incredibly thirsty wild animal, panting after a long, cool drink of water. That's dangerous! Before Eve actually ate the forbidden fruit in the Garden of Eden, she took a good look at it. She looked at it longingly. She admired it. She began to covet it. Then she ate it.

There's something very interesting about covetousness. Although God lists it as idolatry and warns against it in the Ten Commandments, very few people understand what it is. To illustrate this phenomenon, I cite the case of a Roman Catholic priest who had personally heard the confessions of more than two thousand people. Among the sins he heard confessed were lying, stealing, murder, countless cases of adultery—but not a single case of covetousness. That's right—not a single person had listed covetousness among their sins.

Is there something that belongs to another that you secretly covet? Are there possessions that secretly possess *you*? Now is a good time to take an honest inventory.

3. Ourselves. Ultimately, all idolatry comes down to self-worship. People throughout history have wanted to be in control. After all, mankind hasn't changed. People still want to worship something. Why not make a god in our own image and worship it? When we refuse to relinquish control of our lives to God and insist on controlling it ourselves, we are making idols of ourselves. The apostle Paul was speaking of this form of idolatry when he wrote to the church in Rome: "Although they knew God, they did not glorify Him as God, nor were thankful, but became futile in their thoughts, and their foolish hearts were darkened. Professing to be wise, they became fools, and changed the glory of the incorruptible God in to an image made like corruptible man. . . " (Rom. 1:21–23).

In much the same way, some people worship their bodies. People spend hours at the gym, sculpting their bodies, yet completely neglecting their spiritual lives. First Timothy 4:8 says, "Physical training is of some value, but godliness has value for all things, holding promise for both the present life and the life to come" (NIV). Some people think nothing of getting up at the crack of dawn and heading to the gym for that hour-and-a-half workout. But they balk at the idea of spending ten minutes reading the Word of God. They think nothing of sweating 'til their muscles burn, yet they recoil from spending time in prayer. They find time to work out, rain or shine, but if it rains on Sunday, that pouring rain is a really great excuse to skip church. Some people think nothing of working out for hours on a stair-stepper or a treadmill; yet they back down at the thought of building their "spiritual muscles" through the disciplines of prayer and Bible study. They easily accept the pain that comes with completing a 10K run, yet can't see the value of applying themselves to run the race of life.

I suggest that this may mean more than just working to achieve a great set of "pecs." I believe that to these individuals, working out has become an idol or, more specifically, their bodies have become idols. Their bodies have become more important to them than their spiritual lives—which is the real essence of who they are, if they would only come to see it that way.

There is a place for physical exercise and for giving attention to our physical bodies. It helps us to stay healthy and productive, but let's keep it in perspective, shall we? Jesus gave us the blueprint for keeping these—and all things—in perspective when He said, "Seek first the kingdom of God and His righteousness, and all these things shall be added to you" (Matt. 6:33). The phrase "seek first" means to seek principally—above all things—the rule and reign of Christ in one's life. That will keep everything else in the proper balance—even physical exercise.

In another twist to this type of idolatry, untold billions of dollars are being spent today by a culture obsessed with beauty and youth. We don't want wrinkles, so we buy wrinkle cream. We have face-lifts, tummy-tucks, and liposuction. We go on exotic diets. Countless young girls take their fashion clues from overly thin, waif-like models whose faces appear on trendy fashion magazines. In some major cities, nose jobs and other forms of cosmetic surgery are being performed routinely on *teenagers*. Today's teens—unhappy with the way they look due to comparing themselves with these models, rock stars, Hollywood film icons, and other impossible standards of beauty—are flocking in for surgery to change the way they look.

Women aren't the only ones who seem to be obsessed with staying young and attractive. Men, too, are having cosmetic surgery and using a wide array of mens' skin care products in today's youth-conscious culture. Yet it is to female believers that Peter wrote, "Your beauty should not come from outward adornment, such as braided hair and the wearing of gold jewelry and fine clothes. Instead, it should be that of your inner self, the unfading beauty of a gentle and quiet spirit, which is of a great worth in God's sight" (1 Pet. 3:3–4, NIV).

Please don't misunderstand me. I am not saying that you should completely neglect your physical body. I am not saying that the things I have just mentioned are necessarily in and of themselves bad. I am simply pointing out that these things can be symptoms of a deeper problem—the over-emphasis of the physical to the complete neglect of the spiritual. Your body is the temple of the Holy Spirit. Keep yourself in shape, but don't place being in shape—or for that matter, how you look—above God. Keep God first, and He will hold you steady as you jog, pump iron, or do your daily aerobics.

4. Our appetites. Philippians 3:18 (PHILLIPS) states, "There are many . . . [whose lives make them] the enemies of the cross of Christ. These men are heading for utter destruction—their god is their own appetite, their pride is in what they should be ashamed of, and this world is the limit of their horizon." Whatever these individuals want, they take. Remember, physical appetites involve much more than just the hunger for food. They include sensual appetites—the sex drive and physical passions.

Even King Solomon, who was considered to be the wisest man who ever lived, reached a point where he allowed his passions to be released without restraint. For a period of time, he abandoned the principles of faith he had learned at his father's knee. The son of King David and a man of unparalleled wealth and power, King Solomon went on a "binge" that included indulging his every appetite. He later wrote, "Whatever my eyes desired I did not keep from them. I did not withhold my heart from any pleasure . . . Then I looked on all the works that my hands had done . . . And indeed all was vanity . . ." (Eccl. 2:10–11).

Sounds a lot like one famous actor who made millions from the box office receipts of his movies. He told an interviewer, "I feel a void . . . I feel something's missing. I don't think there's anyone who feels like there isn't something missing in their life. No matter how much you accomplish, how much money you make, or how many cars or houses you have, or how many people you make happy, life isn't perfect for anybody."

This type of pleasure-seeking thinking is nothing new. Back in the first century, a group known as the Epicureans believed in a godless, random universe in which atoms came together simply by chance to create everything that's in existence. They did not believe in heaven, hell, or life beyond the grave. Consequently, they did not believe in the judgment of sin. For that matter, they did not believe in sin. They were quite adamant about their belief that man's chief purpose in life was the pursuit of happiness. The lengths they took to achieve it are legend. History records some of the Epicureans' night-long revelings, which included numerous courses of food and drink. So caught up in this pursuit of pleasure were the Epicureans that they took time out from their enjoyment of the foods being served to regurgitate what they had just consumed, thus making it possible to consume even more! What an unappetizing idea! Apparently, "Eat, drink, and be merry!" was their slogan.

Needless to say, this "Epicurean mentality" is still with us today. So many people appear to be living for only the pursuit of pleasure. The Bible, in fact, lists this as one of the distinguishing signs of the days immediately prior to the promised return of Christ. Of this Epicurean mindset, the Bible says, "In the last days . . . men will be lovers of . . . pleasure rather than lovers of God" (2 Tim. 3:1–2, 4).

Today's youth have some pretty strange "idols." They seem to offer hero worship to rock and rap stars, and Hollywood film stars rather than genuine heroes who have risked life and limb to save the lives of others. This is in spite of continual publicity pointing out the emptiness associated with most fame and fortune. One noted Hollywood actor spoke candidly about this "pleasure mania." In an interview, he said, "I found that I couldn't shove enough drugs, women, cars, stereos, houses, and stardom in there to make me feel good. I guess that's why a lot of people overdose—they get to the point where the hole is so big they die."

The late rock star Kurt Cobain is a prime example of this phenomenon. When asked by friends how he was doing, he would reply: "I hate myself and want to die. . . ." At the height of his career as the lead singer in the metal band, Nirvana, he chose suicide. Why? He cited depression, emptiness, lack of purpose in life, and even boredom among his reasons.

The person who bows at the altar of the idol of pleasure can be likened to one who stands in line one day at an amusement park, simply for the opportunity to take a thrill ride that lasts for approximately 2.3 minutes. Then it's back out into the blazing sun to stand in line . . . again. The Bible warns about the futility of such a lifestyle. "She who lives in pleasure is dead while she lives" (1 Tim. 5:6).

Psychologist William Marston once asked three thousand people the question, "What do you live for?" He was shocked to discover that 94 percent of the respondents simply stated that they were enduring the present while waiting for the future. They seemed to be floating, going nowhere. When asked what they were waiting for, some replied that they were waiting for their children to grow up and leave home "so they could have some freedom," while others said they were waiting for the next year, the next windfall, or the next big vacation. Imagine spending life waiting . . . just waiting!

Others spend their lives pursuing sexual gratification. They think they can flagrantly break God's laws without any consequences. I once read a newspaper article about a man who went bungee jumping from a hot-air balloon. There was just one problem: he didn't calculate the distance properly. The bungee cord was too long. Regardless of how many thrills and chills he may have experienced on the way down, it was a one-way trip that cost him his life. He may have even thought, "When is this bungee cord going to break my fall?" It never did.

Likewise, many people today think their promiscuous lifestyles will never catch up with them. The Bible describes this attitude: "Because the sentence against an evil work is not executed speedily, therefore, the heart of the sons of men is fully set in them to do evil" (Eccl. 8:11). Allow me to loosely paraphrase that verse: "When you don't get busted for sin right away, you start to believe that it will never happen." Sooner or later, the Bible says, the punishment for sin will catch up to the crime. "Do not be deceived, God is not mocked; for whatever a man sows, that he will also reap. For he who sows to his flesh will of the flesh reap corruption, but he who sows to the Spirit will of the Spirit reap everlasting life" (Gal. 6:7–8).

Today's teens are especially careless in this regard. Dr. Karen Hein of New York's Albert Einsten College of Medicine said, "This is the first AIDS generation. Youth feel invulnerable. They don't believe this is going to happen to them. . . ."[2]

The AIDS virus took the life of rock star Freddy Mercury, lead singer in the band, Queen. After discovering that he had AIDS, Mercury—who knew he did not have long to live—took a long, hard look at his life and its purpose, and brought those thoughts together in a song called "Party," featured on the group's 1989 album, *The Miracle*. The lyrics included these lines:

> "We were up all night singing and giving a chase,
> but in the cold light of day the next morning,
> the party was over."[3]

Then the song breaks into a refrain that implores Mercury's party-mates:

"Come back and play . . . come back and play."[4]

The album grows dark from there.

I recall watching a video of one of Queen's last concerts. The camera recorded a stunning shot of Freddy Mercury, microphone in hand, singing to a literal sea of "worshipers," whose hands were held high in homage to their god of music. How tragic. Not too long after that, he was dead.

5. *Our children.* Is it possible that Abraham at one time made an idol out of his beloved son, Isaac? I personally believe this is so. After all, he had waited so long for this child of promise—this child born in his old age who brought Abraham and Sarah so much joy.

Many years before the birth of Isaac, God had promised Abraham a son. But Abraham and his wife, Sarah, grew impatient. They were getting older. By now Sarah was well past the age of child-bearing capability. If they were going to have a son, it seemed to them that they would have to help God out. So they took matters into their own hands. Sarah suggested that Abraham have sexual relations with her handmaid, Hagar. Then she and Abraham would raise the child. That way, Abraham's seed would continue throughout the generations. It didn't take long after Hagar gave birth to Abraham's son, Ishmael, for each party involved to realize they had made a horrible mistake. Abraham soon realized that his desperate plan was not the will of God at all.

More time passed. Finally, just when it seemed truly impossible, Sarah became pregnant. She gave birth to Isaac, just as God had promised. Isaac was the physical representation of everything Abraham held dear. He was the child of promise—a physical link to the coming Messiah. As he watched Isaac grow from a toddler into a young boy, his love for his son grew. It is quite possible that at one point, Abraham—the friend of God—actually began to love Isaac a little bit more than he loved God.

At this point, God tested Abraham. "He said, 'Take now your son, your only son Isaac, whom you love, and go to the land of

Moriah, and offer him there as a burnt offering. . . " (Gen. 22:2). Just to show that Abraham had his priorities straight, he obeyed. When challenged with giving up what he loved most in the world, Abraham set a biblical example for believers who came after him. He obediently took Isaac up to the place where God had told him to sacrifice his son. Abraham knew that the God he loved would, if necessary, even resurrect his son from the dead.

We know the rest of the story—how God sent an angel to deliver Isaac from the blade his father held poised over him. At the last moment God spared the life of Isaac.

We must love our children, but we must be careful not to idolize them. God requires first place in our hearts.

6. *Television.* Several years ago, my wife, Cathe, and I spent some time walking around Balboa Island in Newport Beach. The people who live on Balboa Island have beautiful homes overlooking the water. Many of these people keep their curtains open at night, so when people walk by, they can see straight into their homes. We could see people eating dinner or playing cards as we walked by. As Cathe and I progressed down the boardwalk, we noticed that most of the people sat inside homes that seemed to be illuminated by a strange blue light. In home after home, we saw dozens of people glued to—you guessed it—their television sets. They seemed to be immersed in some form of high worship. They sat in their darkened rooms, the television's blue haze reflecting flickering images across the walls or glinting off the windows. Sometimes this strange glow even captured the mesmerized expressions on the faces of the viewers. They didn't appear to be talking to one another. We could see no movement from room to room. The inhabitants just seemed to sit there like statues, bathed in eerie, blue light.

A recent Nielsen survey of the television viewing habits of Americans revealed that women over the age of fifty-five spend almost thirty-six hours a week in front of "the tube." That's thirty-six hours a week of Geraldo, Oprah, Donahue, and their favorite soaps. It also revealed that children under the age of six watch twenty-seven hours of television per week. The average American family spends six hours and forty-four minutes a day watching television. One journalist has suggested that if someone from another planet landed on earth and attempted to beam an urgent message to reach the largest number of "earthlings" at one time, the best time would be on a Sunday night in November between 8:30 and 9:00 P.M. That's when nearly 100 percent of all the households in the United States would have their television sets turned on. Imagine that!

7. *Money.* The Bible speaks about those who constantly desire to be rich. Ironically, this does not mean just those who are rich. What about the person who makes very little money but who is constantly coming up with some "get rich quick" scheme that places a steady drain on the finances that he does have coming in. Perhaps it's lottery tickets. This person will even have a rationale for spending too much on lottery tickets. "I'm just supporting the local school system!" How about the person who constantly blows money in Las Vegas casinos—always looking to hit "the big one." These individuals are looking for a "quick fix," hoping for a break, and searching for a shortcut. They are obsessed with being millionaires.

And there are plenty of people out there who will tell you how to strike it rich. Late-night television airwaves are jammed with people sharing their schemes for overnight financial success. A person who is obsessed with riches may have very little in his or her bank account. Yet this person may be more materialistic than someone who is worth millions.

In describing what happened to the seed that fell among weeds in the parable of the sower and the seed, Jesus said, "The cares of this world, the deceitfulness of riches, and the desires for other things entering in choke the word [the seed], and it becomes unfruitful" (Mark 4:19). Along the same lines, Paul warned, "Those who desire to be rich fall into temptation and a snare. . . . For the love of money is a root of all kinds of evil, for which some have strayed from the faith in their greediness [or covetousness], and pierced themselves through with many sorrows" (1 Tim. 6:9–10).

Please allow me to make a distinction here: it is quite possible to be very well off and not have a problem with this form of idolatry. On the other hand, it is very possible to have very little, but struggle with it daily.

To some people, having a lot of money is not idolatry. To others, *not having much money* is!

The Insidiousness of Idolatry

Idolatry is really quite insidious. It usually happens slowly, over the passage of time. Little by little, the changeover from truth to error takes place . . . compromise by compromise. I once heard the story of a man who was upset over the high cost of the oats he fed to his mule. Gradually, he began to substitute sawdust in the animal's diet. Everything seemed to be going along fine—until the day the mule keeled over. The mule, finally satisfied with his sawdust diet, had a full stomach—but had received no nourishment. He died.

That's how it is with idolatry.

Have you ever wondered, like I have, how the Israelites could have traded in a vital relationship with the God of the manna and the miracles and the pillars of smoke and fire for a few pounds of gold, shaped into the likeness of a calf? Again, it is important to note that the changeover didn't take place all at once. It happened gradually over a period of time—the result of a series of compromises.

That's how it happens yet today.

There is an Antidote

Did you know that there is an antidote for idolatry? The best antidote I know of is a passionate, committed, close relationship with Jesus Christ. When we walk closely with Him, we won't want any other gods. We won't allow other things or people to crowd Him out. We will be able to say, as Paul did, "For to me, to live is Christ . . ." (Phil. 1:21).

That doesn't mean we don't care about other things. That doesn't mean we shouldn't have a life. What it means is that everything else falls into place in its order of importance *after* our relationship with Christ. We will then find that we are no longer interested in cheap imitations and distractions.

LET'S PRAY

Have you been struggling with idolatry in some area of your life? If the answer is "yes," why not make a clean break with it now and pray a prayer something like this one?

Father, I thank You for pointing out to me the areas in my life where I have fallen into the compromise of idolatry. I repent and ask You to forgive me. Please cleanse me of idolatry in every area of my life, and help me to keep myself from idols as I continue my walk with You. Thank You for Your mercy and for Your compassionate restoration. In Jesus' name, I pray. Amen.

6

REMEMBER LOT'S WIFE

But [*Lot's*] wife looked back behind him, and she became a pillar of salt.

—*Genesis 19:26*

Have you ever left something at home that you were supposed to take with you? Your wallet? Watch? Purse? Driver's license? Briefcase?

If you're like me, remembering what you forgot often happens behind the steering wheel of your car as you're headed for work. You're about fifteen minutes from home. Suddenly you remember: "Oh, no! I forgot so and so!" As frustration gives way to anger, you wonder, "Why didn't I think of that when I was just *one* minute away from home?" Now you're going to have to turn around and go back.

It's amazing how things flit in and out of our memories, often at the oddest times.

You're just getting ready to doze off to sleep. Suddenly you sit straight up in bed, wide awake. "Oh, no! I forgot to do _____!" You fill in the blank.

We've all been there.

Sometimes we're the ones who need to be reminded to do certain things, and sometimes it's our responsibility to remind others. For example, I have to remind my two sons, Jonathan and Christopher, to do things from time to time. For my oldest son, Christopher, it's usually, "Remember to take out the trash." Invariably, he will say, "Aw, Dad—not now! I'll do it in a few minutes!" I remind him again and again as those "few minutes" stretch into hours. Finally he falls asleep—and *I* have to take out the trash! I don't know where it's written, but isn't there a law that says men must always take out the trash? Wherever this law originated, I have come to accept it. I have also come to accept that it's my prerogative as a father *to pass the buck to my sons!* I'm getting my youngest son, Jonathan, started on the "First Law of Trash" at an early age. But I'm still having trouble convincing Christopher that trash duty will be one of his lifelong priorities.

Lest you think I never have to remind Jonathan to do anything, I must admit that I have to remind him to do a few things too. I'll say to Jonathan, "Remember to come home in thirty minutes," or, "Remember to brush your teeth before you go to bed."

Why must I remember to tell my sons these things? Why must we remind anyone of anything at all? Because we have a tendency to forget. All too often, it seems that we remember what we ought to forget . . . and forget what we should have remembered.

Has that ever happened to you?

Jesus' Reminder to His Flock

Jesus knew our tendency to forget things. So in Luke, chapter 17, He reminded us of something important—something we should remember and apply to the last days.

> Just as it was in the days of Noah, so also will it be in the days of the Son of Man. People were eating, drinking, marrying and being given in marriage up to the day Noah entered the ark. Then the flood came and destroyed them all. It was the same in the days of Lot. People were eating and drinking, buying and selling, planting and building. But the day Lot left Sodom, fire and sulfur rained down from heaven and destroyed them all. It will be just like this on the day the Son of Man is revealed. On that day no one who is on the roof of his house, with his goods inside, should go down to get them. Likewise, no one in the field should go back for anything. *Remember Lot's wife!* Whoever tries to keep his life will lose it, and whoever loses his life will preserve it.
>
> —Luke 17:26–33, NIV, italics mine

Remember Lot's wife. What a curious statement! Amid all this talk about the last days, as Jesus describes the conditions on earth prior to His return, He just tosses in this warning: "Remember Lot's wife!" At a glance, it almost doesn't seem to fit. But when we examine it in the context of making a comparison between the morality of Noah's time and Lot's time and *the end time,* it's not hard to make a clear connection. Jesus clearly drew a parallel. Then He added a warning.

When we consider Noah's time, we think of violence. Excessive wickedness, cruelty, and bloodshed marked that time in biblical history. According to the Bible, the earth was filled with so much violence that God was sorry He had even made man (see Gen. 6:5–6). Drive-by shootings, a steady diet of bloody and violent television programming and movies, rioting, drug deals gone bad, mass murders, gang activity, the robbing and killing of tourists, horrible episodes of child abuse—these are just some of the violent acts occurring today in our nation alone. That doesn't even begin to cover the killing going on in Bosnia, the continual violence in different parts of Africa, or the powder-keg conditions in the Middle East.

When we look at Lot's time, we see a generation characterized by sexual perversion. We, too, are living in times of great perversion. People have twisted God's natural design for men and women into something other than simply being joined together in marriage. Rampant homosexuality, various crimes against children, the wholesale availability of hardcore pornography, the deterioration of any moral code whatsoever in the production of films and television, sexually loose lifestyles— again, these are just a few examples of just how perverse our culture has become.

In both these cases, God brought judgment upon the people. In the time of Noah, that judgment came by water—a mighty deluge that wiped all traces of mankind from the earth, with the exception of faithful Noah, his family, and an ark filled with numerous animals. In Lot's time, the judgment was by fire and brimstone which fell suddenly from heaven, completely annihilating the cities of Sodom and Gomorrah. And in both cases, the people of the day were unprepared for the judgment of God. They ate. They drank. They bought. They sold. They married.

They conducted business as usual, entirely oblivious to the coming destruction. Both Noah and Lot attempted to warn those around them of the judgment that was about to take place. But in each case, their warnings were considered to be empty religious ravings.

Jesus drew parallels between the time of Noah, the time of Lot, and the end time to create a vivid description of the deteriorated spiritual climate on earth at the time of His return. Why, then, did He include the seemingly incongruent statement, *"Remember Lot's wife"*? To warn His flock of the subtle, erosive influences of compromise.

Lot, the Compromiser

The Bible doesn't have very much to say about Lot's wife. We are not even told her name. She is simply referred to, in Genesis, chapter 19, as "Lot's wife." But we do know quite a bit about Lot. Understanding a few important things about Lot, I believe, will provide greater insight into understanding his wife—her values, her beliefs, her background, and what it was about her that Jesus wanted us to remember.

Lot was the nephew of Abraham—the only man identified in the Bible as the intimate "friend of God." Abraham, that great man of faith, had a close, personal relationship with his Creator. He walked with God. Lot really admired Uncle Abraham. He liked to be around him . . . liked the kind of man he was. Abraham walked with God, but Lot walked with Abraham. In other words, while Abraham had a very special relationship with God, Lot's relationship with God was contingent on his relationship with his uncle. He was free-loading. He was just going along for the ride, living off the faith of Abraham, instead of developing his own unique relationship with God.

Lot discovered how easy it was to let his uncle do the praying and the intercession. It seemed that Uncle Abraham was constantly going to bat for him with God. Each time Lot found himself entangled in some type of trouble, there was Uncle Abraham—to the rescue. Compromise!

Lot loved the world too much. When his uncle moved the tribe to Egypt, Lot loved it! Civilization! Sophisticated culture! Colorful history! Elaborate cities! Exotic foods! When Uncle

Abraham decided to return to the plains of Israel, Lot was disappointed. Just when he was getting used to city life!

As Abraham prospered, so did Lot. Their possessions grew, as
did their flocks. At home again in Israel, trouble broke out between their herdsmen. In addition, constant friction had begun
to develop between Lot and Abraham. Abraham viewed the
plains of Israel as the land of his inheritance, while Lot missed
Egypt and longed for the excitement and adventure of city life.
Abraham was oriented to pleasing God, but Lot was oriented to
pleasing himself. The Bible poses the question, "Do two walk
together unless they have agreed to do so?" (Amos 3:3, NIV). In
the midst of all this strife, God began to deal with Abraham
about making a break with Lot. Abraham had been dragging his
feet. Finally one day Abraham went to Lot and said, "Listen,
buddy, we've got to part company. I'll tell you what—you decide
where you want to go. If you want to go to the right, I'll go to
the left. You want to go to the left? I'll go to the right. You want
to go south? I'll go north. You just choose your place and I'll go
the other way."

Now the ball was totally in Lot's court. The "city boy" in him
came surging to the surface. "Hey," Lot exclaimed, filled with
fresh excitement at the prospect of a bright future. "I've been
checking out this one place, and it really looks good to me.
Sodom and Gomorrah! That's where I'd like to live!"

That was his first mistake. The Bible records that this place was
filled with perversion and every wicked thing. The Bible also
states that when Lot looked toward these two cities, he "looked
with longing." Have you ever seen someone do that? A kid with
his face pressed to a candy store window . . . a young person
checking out a shiny, new, red sports car . . . "Oooo, I want *that*
for *me!*" That's the way Lot looked at Sodom and Gomorrah.

Then he moved closer. He moved right out to the fringe. In
another step down into compromise, Lot "pitched his tent toward
Sodom." By now, he had undoubtedly become fascinated by the
free-wheeling lifestyles of the Sodomites. They disregarded God.
They did exactly as they pleased. Lot may have even thought,
"Hey, maybe I can go over there and make a difference for God!
Now, I don't want to be too preachy, and I don't want to push
anything on anyone. I'll just kind of blend in. I'll just be one of

the gang. I'll just relate to them and slowly but surely, I'll turn them around. Eventually, they'll come around to what I believe."

Sure they will.

Famous last words.

Lot, the "Mugwump"

Lot's problem was that he was a classic *mugwump*. What is a "mugwump?" A "mugwump" is a fence-sitter. A "mugwump," in fact, is someone who sits on a fence with his "mug" on one side and his "wump" on the other.

"Mugwumps" are fascinated with the world and what it has to offer. They love "stuff." They love excitement. They love self-gratification.

In my opinion, Lot was a such a person. He tried to have it both ways—he tried to live in two worlds. Isn't it the same with many Christians today?

They want to be Christians. They want the assurance of knowing they will one day spend eternity in heaven. They want Jesus Christ in their lives—but they also want to do what everyone else is doing. They want to party. They want to have fun. They want to blend in. They don't want to make any sacrifices. They don't want to give up anything. They want it all—and they want it all their way.

Have you met anyone who fits this description? One day it's, "Oh, God is so good! Praise the Lord! I'm serving Him!" And the next day it's, "I haven't got time for church! I've got to party! I've got to have a life, after all!" Up and down, down and up, up and down, and back and forth. Now it's church. Now it's the world. Up and down. Up and down. It just won't work. This type of "yo-yo Christianity" will eventually play itself out.

People who play this game are usually very miserable. They have too much of the world in them to be happy in the Lord, and too much of the Lord in them to be happy in the world.

The Bible says, "Choose for yourselves this day whom you will serve. . ." (Josh. 24:15). Sooner or later "mugwumps" will have to decide which side of the fence they prefer. God has a habit of shaking the fence just enough to force a decision. Will it be the things of God or the things of this world? Every "mugwump" must eventually decide.

Are *you* a "mugwump?"

God Sends a Warning

Soon after Lot settled in Sodom, the Bible records an interesting development. He and his family were taken hostage by a king who made war against the Sodomites. Lot and his family could have died in captivity, but once more good old Uncle Abraham came to the rescue! Leading a small band of men in a bold little military raid, Uncle Abraham and his men delivered Lot and his entire family. This temporary captivity was a warning from God, saying, "Don't go back to Sodom and Gomorrah! Don't lower your standards! Don't compromise!"

But Lot missed the point. How did he respond to his good fortune? Did he heed the warning from God? No. He simply said, "Thanks, Uncle Abraham!" Perhaps he even reasoned, "And to show you how grateful I am to you for rescuing me, I'm going back there and I'm going to lead these Sodomites to God! I'm going to become established there. I'm going to make a difference. I'll be an influence for good."

The last time we hear of Lot, he is a leader in Sodom and Gomorrah. He is sitting in the gates. He has joined the club. How unfortunate!

Have you ever been going in the wrong direction when God sends a warning to stop you, turn you around, and get you going in the right direction again? No doubt, that's what God intended to do in Lot's case. When Abraham led him out of captivity, Lot had a chance to leave the wickedness of Sodom and Gomorrah behind. Instead, he chose to return to the place that would later be visited by the judgment of God.

Warnings can come in many ways, can't they? Sometimes it's easy for us to understand God's warnings in our daily lives. But sometimes those warnings may need to be a little more direct.

Perhaps you are in the theater at a local mall, waiting in line to purchase a ticket to the latest hot new film—the one that barely received an "R" rating because of its strong sexual content. There you are—about to go into that theater to see a film that your conscience has been telling you that you really shouldn't see—when a Christian brother spots you. You think, "Oh, great! Maybe if I pretend I don't see him, he'll just go away!" No such luck! He hurries over and starts a conversation.

He says, "Hey, brother, how are you doing?" You mumble something as the line inches closer to the ticket booth. You say to yourself, "I can't believe this!" He just continues to stand there as the person in the ticket booth asks which film you wish to see. Now you're going to have to ask for the ticket within this guy's earshot. "Uh. . . . Is *Bambi* showing tonight?"

What will you do? Will you take the hint? Will you choose to see another movie? Or will you go ahead, ignore the warning, and choose the film that you really know you shouldn't see? Situations like these are not coincidental. I firmly believe they are orchestrated by the Lord.

Some warnings are stronger than others. In this day of rampant, sexually transmitted diseases, wholesale abortion, and the AIDS epidemic, there have never been more reasons to teach sexual abstinence before marriage. Yet some people—often young people—persist in leading sexually loose lifestyles. How about the girl who has been leading such a lifestyle, and who one day fears she's pregnant? Inside, she knows that what she's been doing is wrong. Her parents raised her in church, and she clearly knows the difference between right and wrong. She begins to "bargain" with God: "Oh, please—help me! God, I'm reaching out to You! If You'll just help me, I'll go back to church! I'll serve You!" But when she discovers that she is not pregnant, she forgets her part of the "bargain." She returns to her former lifestyle, as if to say, "*Adios,* God—see You next crisis!" She ignores God's warning.

Perhaps the warning is a little stronger. How about the guy who has been leading a fast lifestyle. Drugs, sex, no limits. One day he gets the flu . . . and it doesn't go away. He's heard the stories about how AIDS symptoms begin to appear. Now he's frantic. "Oh, no! I've got AIDS!" Here is your basic, self-made man, scared to death. All the money, all the success in the world can't buy him out of this jam. He begins to cry out to God: "Oh, God! I'll serve You! I'll do anything! I'm sorry! I won't do it again. I'll clean up my act. I'll go into the mission field if that's what You want me to do!" Then the results of his test return and he discovers that he doesn't have AIDS after all. Does he heed the warning? Does he honor his commitment to God? No. He returns to his former lifestyle.

Some people never get the message. Lot didn't get the message either. He could have said, "What am I doing, going back to Sodom and Gomorrah? This is ridiculous!" But Lot—like so many people today—had become intoxicated by the allure of sin.

Never Underestimate the Power of Sin

You may say, "Oh, I can handle it!" You may say, "I can stop anytime I want!" You may say, "I'm a Christian! I've been walking with the Lord for ten years! I'm in control!" But I have seen too many examples of the way sin takes people down to believe any of these flimsy excuses. Never underestimate the intoxicating power of sin! I repeat—*never underestimate the intoxicating power of sin!* Regardless of how long you've been walking with the Lord, or how strong your walk with Him is, or how many Scripture verses you may have committed to memory, sin still has the power to obscure the difference between following God and following evil.

You may say, "I know when to quit. It'll stop right here. . . ." Come on! Wise up! It doesn't happen that way.

One day, you find yourself in the pit and you say, "How did I get down here?" You underestimated the power of sin. You played with it. You thought you could control it. That's why the Bible says, "Abstain from all appearance of evil" (1 Thess. 5:22, KJV). Keep it at a distance. If you don't, you may be sorry. Sin has brought down some of the strongest men and women who ever lived. Be careful.

Lot was not careful. He went back to Sodom and Gomorrah. He became a leader there. It cost him his spiritual edge. He became so spiritually dull that he no longer realized how bad things had become there. Sin had finally worn him down. Peter wrote this about Lot: "He was completely worn down by the manner of life of the lawless and the realm of unbridled lust" (2 Pet. 2:8, PHILLIPS). Lot had gotten used to the steadily deteriorating conditions of day-to-day life in Sodom and Gomorrah.

Again Abraham went to bat for Lot. He prayed for Lot and his whole family. He asked God to have mercy on Sodom and Gomorrah. And once again, God answered Abraham's prayer. He sent two angels into Sodom and Gomorrah to deliver Lot and his family from the coming judgment.

God Sends His Messengers

When Lot saw the two strangers, he bowed down before them. Perhaps something about them reminded him of Uncle Abraham. It was not so much that their faces seemed to shine radiantly—it was more the look in their eyes. Were they angels? Lot suspected so. He had heard his uncle tell of angels. "Come home with me and be my honored guests!" Lot invited. But the angels said, "We would rather sleep in the street." Lot persisted in urging the men to accompany him to his home for the night, and finally they relented.

Why was Lot so adamantly against the men sleeping outside, in the open? The reason became apparent when the men of the city completely surrounded Lot's house and demanded that he send the two strangers out to them. The Bible says, "All the men from every part of the city of Sodom—both young and old—surrounded the house. They called to Lot, 'Where are the men who came to you tonight? Bring them out to us, so that we can have sex with them'" (Gen. 19:4–5 , NIV). The male inhabitants had become so perverse that whenever strangers came to town, they demanded to have sex with them! Rampant homosexual sin! Lot—usually dulled by the presence of this sin—was embarrassed by it in the presence of these angelic visitors.

In an incredible compromise, Lot went to the men gathered outside and said, "Brothers, don't be so wicked! Friends, don't do this!" *Earth to Lot! Brothers? Friends?* You must be kidding!

Then Lot made a truly horrible offer: "Take my two daughters! They have never known a man. Do with them as you please, but leave these two men alone." The men of Sodom and Gomorrah would not be satisfied with such a counter-offer. They wanted the men. As they began to push and shove and force their way into Lot's home, the angels stepped forth and said, "We'll take care of this!"

They smote the men with blindness. But these men were so far gone in their perversion that even though blinded, they still groped for the door. So blinded by their sins were they that they still wanted what they had come for, in spite of the judgment that had just been visited upon them.

The angels had seen enough. They said to Lot, "Get your wife. Get your daughters. Get your family. We're getting out of here." As Lot's wife reluctantly prepared to leave, Lot wanted to warn his sons-in-law.

When Lot told them about the coming judgment, they thought he was joking. "Come on," he said. "God's judgment is about to fall! We've got to get out of here! Here—these two angels will take us to safety!" How could his sons-in-law be expected to take Lot seriously? They had watched him compromise so often and repeatedly lower his standards so that his witness had long since lost its authority.

What Does All This Have to Do with Lot's Wife?

Now, you may say, "Greg—that's nice. You've told us all about Lot. But what about Lot's wife? Jesus said, 'Remember Lot's wife.' When are you going to tell us about her?"

As I mentioned earlier, the Bible doesn't have much to say about her. But let's put together what we know. We don't really know where she came from, but I think we can safely assume that Lot met his wife after he moved to Sodom. Therefore, we may also assume that she was a non-believer. In that case, Lot was unequally yoked in marriage. She probably pulled him in her direction more than Lot pulled her in his direction.

Apparently, this woman liked living in Sodom. When it came time to flee the city, she went along reluctantly. How many times throughout their marriage had there been conflict when Lot wanted to proceed in a certain way, but his wife dragged her feet? The conflict they experienced on the night of their escape from Sodom again underscores God's warning: "Do not be unequally yoked together with unbelievers. . . " (2 Cor. 6:14).

But what does that mean? People ask me that all the time! Okay, let me put it this way: one obvious application would be "Don't marry a non-believer!" That seems obvious to many, but you would be surprised how many people have come to me on this one issue—and I would have to admit, more girls than guys—trying to find some way around the truth of this passage of text. "Well, the Lord has just brought us together and we're really in love and. . . . " *Is he a Christian?* "Uh, you know, I . . . I think he goes to church, uh . . . Easter . . . ten years ago.

He says 'God' a lot! Yeah, I think he kind of, probably, sort of is. . . . "

Anyone considering marriage with a non-believer has a problem. Not only should Christians be looking for a mate who names the name of Christ as Savior, but they should be searching for a godly man or a woman. In God's order, the man must be the spiritual leader in the home and the woman must be a godly woman. The Bible says, "Who can find a virtuous woman? For her price is far above rubies. . . . Favour is deceitful, and beauty is vain: but a woman that feareth the Lord, she shall be praised" (Prov. 31:10, 30, KJV).

My advice to single men and women who wish to marry is this: wait on God's timing. Pray and continue to believe God for His best, and He will bring the right girl or the right guy to you. If you get in a hurry and marry an unbeliever, you'll be making a big mistake. You'll be yoked together for life. I suggest you heed the advice of one of the founding fathers of the United States, Benjamin Franklin, who said, "Keep your eyes open before marriage and half shut afterwards."

A *yoke* is a wooden device which was used to hook two animals together to pull a plow or wagon or some other type of conveyance. In what direction do you think the yoke will pull if you yoke a live cow with a dead one? It will always pull downward in the direction of that which is dead. The dead animal will prove to be a stumbling block for the living animal as it tries to make progress and accomplish the task it is assigned to perform.

In much the same way, the spiritually alive person is dragged down when yoked with one who is spiritually dead—the non-believer. Why? Because the believer still has an old, dead nature, but the non-believer does not have a new nature. In that case, it's a lot easier to go backward than forward. It's a bit like parking a car on a hill, then putting it into neutral. Which way will the car roll? Downhill!

So it appears that Lot was unequally yoked. It's no wonder he was such a miserable man. Try as he might to blend in, he just couldn't do it. While Lot's wife probably supported him, no doubt she saw his inner struggle. She probably said to Lot, "Hey, you're so guilt-ridden! Lighten up! Have a little fun!" But Lot's guilt only grew. He had begun to make a series of small compromises, failing to realize that such small compromises invariably get out of hand.

Nevertheless, the New Testament lists Lot as a righteous man. God had once been a part of Lot's life. Although he had compromised numerous times, although he had repeatedly lowered his standards, deep down in his heart he wanted to do what was right.

His wife, however, was less enthusiastic about the things of God. Stop and think about her for a moment. She had been exposed to the Word of God through marriage to Lot. She had been exposed to the power of God. Angels came to her town. She saw the miraculous way the men of Sodom were struck blind in judgment of their wickedness. Yet she did not believe.

Over and over in the pages of the Bible, we read of those who were exposed to spiritual things but who did not respond personally in any significant way. There is the story of a man named Gehazi, who was the assistant to one of the greatest men in the Old Testament—the prophet Elisha. God worked many miracles through this prophet, yet Gehazi allowed greed and deception to creep into his life and he was eventually destroyed.

A man named Demas is mentioned in the New Testament. He had as his friend none other than one of the greatest preachers and teachers in church history—the apostle Paul. Paul once referred to Demas as a fellow-worker and a friend. But Demas loved the world more than he loved God, and later Paul referred to him as "Demas, who loved this present world, and deserted me."

There was the Egyptian Pharaoh, who repeatedly saw miracles performed through Moses and Aaron. He saw the Nile River turn to blood. He saw around-the-clock darkness blanket the land for three days. He saw plagues of boils and frogs and lice. Yet he refused to believe. He saw a staff become a snake and witnessed many other incredible things, but his heart only grew harder.

Finally there was the man whose betrayal was the most unbelievable of all—Judas Iscariot. He had actually lived with, walked with, talked with, and eaten with Christ. He heard the great sermons. He saw the numerous miracles. He knew for a fact that Jesus had not sinned. Yet he sold the Savior out for thirty paltry pieces of silver.

So it was with Lot's wife. She had been exposed to the Word of God. She was given the opportunity of deliverance from God's judgment of sin. Yet she threw it all away.

It has been said that the same sun that softens the wax hardens the clay. Every person must determine which it shall be—a heart of wax or a heart of clay? A heart open to the gospel or resistant to what God has to say? Which shall it be?

Those of you who come from Christian homes should pay special heed to this snare called compromise. You could very easily fall into it. You have been accustomed to the things of God since childhood. Yet if you aren't careful, you may begin to take those privileges for granted. You were fortunate enough to be raised in a godly home where scriptural principles were taught and practiced. You were not raised in an abusive home. Be careful! Don't take those things for granted and start lowering your standards. Don't start to compromise a little here and a little there. A little less time in Scripture. Come to church when it's convenient. Spend more time doing other things. Relax the grip. Fall away. Remember Lot's wife!

You may say, "Well, what did she do that was so bad? I mean, all she did was look back and—that was it!—she became a pillar of salt!" But it wasn't simply looking back that was so sinful. It was that her heart was still in Sodom and Gomorrah. She didn't want to leave. Then there is that phrase again which, when translated, we see means, "She looked back *with longing*." She loved it back there! She lingered behind.

Press Forward, Don't Look Back

Remember Lot's wife! Her problem was that she looked back. Jesus said, "No man, having looked back, is fit for the kingdom of heaven" (see Luke 9:62). The apostle Paul had many reasons to look back and find himself unfit for Christian service. Prior to his dynamic conversion on the road to Damascus, he was none other than Saul of Tarsus—a fearsome Pharisee who arrested, tortured, and killed many Christians. How easily he could have been destroyed by his past. How easily he could have felt unusable and have said to himself, "I could never do anything for God! Look at all the horrible things I've done!" But Paul realized, "I can't change what I've done, but I can change what I'm doing."

So Paul wrote this to believers who would follow in the faith: "This one thing I do, forgetting those things which are behind, and reaching forth unto those things which are before, I press toward the mark for the prize of the high calling of God in Christ Jesus" (Phil. 3:13–14, KJV).

Lot's wife was so close to being saved from the judgment. She got out of Sodom. She even had an angelic escort. She was free. She could have said, "I'm out! This is it!" But she left against her will. She didn't want to go. The angels had to take hold of her hands and drag her out to safety. Then, despite a clear warning from the angels not to look back, she turned her head toward Sodom and Gomorrah, and the judgment fell.

Remember Lot's wife! You can't live in the past. This is now! What are you doing right now for Jesus Christ? Are you on fire for Him as you were once on fire? Does that same zeal burn within you? Does that vision for a lifetime of Christian service still determine the direction of your life? Or have you allowed— like Lot did—a series of small compromises to enter in and change the course of your future? Are you walking with Him today? That's all that matters.

Have you been slipping backwards? Have you been lowering your standards? Have you been compromising? Remember Lot's wife! She played games. Remember her! She missed out. Take heed to what happened to her. Don't let it happen to you!

LET'S PRAY

Are you living in the present, or looking back? The "good old days" weren't so great, in the light of eternity, were they? If you've been struggling with the compromise of looking back instead of moving forward, will you pray with me?

Father, I confess that I have been clinging to the past. Please forgive me, as I repent of that compromise now. Help me to look to You, toward the future, and to move forward in the direction in which You lead me. Increase my faith and trust in You. In Jesus' name, I pray. Amen.

7

THE SNARE OF ADULTERY

You shall not commit adultery.

—Exodus 20:14

It's after midnight. Your wife has taken the kids to visit her parents for a week. You're all alone in that great big house. Everything seems so quiet without them. You just microwaved "dinner for one." Now you can't sleep. You reach for the remote control to the television set. Maybe a little late-night "channel surfing" will help. So, with your finger on the button, you flick quickly from one channel to the next, noticing the crummy late-night television fare. Lots of "info-mercials." A couple of shopping networks. CNN Headline News. No—news won't do. What you're looking for is something with a plot, a storyline. There's the usual "get-rich-quick" programming, which never interests you—regardless of what time of day it is. You flick past the dial-a-psychics, and also decide to pass on old reruns of Bonanza and a late-night talk show hosted by a personality that you could take or leave. Now you're into the pay channels. You know the programming on pay channels gets pretty raunchy this late at night. You know—those are the channels that you tell yourself you keep paying for because they feature recently released PG and PG13 movies "for the family," during prime-time hours.

But it's not prime time now. Your conscience says, "Watch it!" But your eyes, lighting on images of a couple locked in the throes of heated passion, are also telling you, *Watch it!*, in direct contrast to those soul-deep warnings being telegraphed.

So you do just that—watch it. After all, who'll ever know? It's just you, all alone there in front of the tube. It doesn't take long before you realize that this steamy tale is about a man who claims to have found fulfillment—even excitement—via an illicit romance. Sure, he's married. So are you. You tell yourself you don't approve. You tell yourself it's against your moral values. You tell yourself it's only a story. What's a little compromise now and then? You tell yourself that by just watching a story like that on TV, you really aren't sinning. Are you?

If it's OK to watch such stuff, why don't you like to watch movies about adultery with your spouse? Why does it make you feel so. . . . ? And afterwards, why is there that feeling in the pit of your stomach that although your moral code is offended by the "A-word," you may secretly be wondering why there isn't more passion in your love life. You aren't *missing something* . . . are you? And just when was it that you began to compare your wife of twenty years with the young, beautiful women whose sleek images have recently been flashing across the "TV screen" of your mind? When did you notice that you were bored?

Fictional scenarios like these are more real than you may think. Remember that old song from the 70s—*Just one look—that's all it took?* Well, so many times that's how it is. All it takes is *just one look* for well-meaning, God-fearing Christians to fall into the snare of adultery.

David and Bathsheba

One look—that's all it took for King David to fall into the snare of adultery. As you know, he was one of Israel's greatest kings ever. The Bible describes him as a "mighty man of valor," and "a man after God's own heart." Then how could such a horrendous thing as an adulterous affair with a married woman have happened to this godly man?

I want to stress the fact that King David did not fall into the compromise of adultery all at once. It happened step by step, little by little, over the passage of time. That's how it happens today.

"Saul has slain his thousands, and David his ten thousands!" That's what the people once sang about David, their king, ever since, as a boy, he slew the giant Philistine warrior known as Goliath. In a matter of minutes, a young, courageous shepherd boy had done with a slingshot what an entire army outfitted with swords and spears could not do. God was glorified as David felled Goliath with a single stone launched from his simple slingshot. With that act of faith and valor, a boy met his destiny. The course of his life was changed forever.

Now, many years later, with many more exciting victories to his credit, the middle-aged warrior king had reached a plateau. He had already accomplished more in his lifetime—a lifetime that was only half over—than some people ever dreamed of accomplishing. Perhaps he was weary. Could it also be that he had become bored by his successes . . . numbed by the adulation of his armies and the people? Was he experiencing the Old Testament equivalent of a mid-life crisis? Whatever his reasons were, David opted out during this particular time when the rest of his men went down to the heat of battle. After all, he had personally trained and appointed his captains. Why should he go down to battle? Instead of sleeping in tents on the battlefield, David was at home, living luxuriously, with plenty of time on his hands.

One balmy, spring evening, the king simply could not sleep. He kept tossing and turning until finally, he rose from bed and walked out onto his royal terrace for a breath of fresh air. But he received a whole lot more than a breath of fresh air that evening. Although he didn't realize it, the king was about to step into another situation that would again change his life forever.

From the vantage point of his rooftop porch—high above the city of Jerusalem—King David could see for miles in every direction. As he looked across the way, his eyes settled upon a scene that made his blood churn. There in plain sight was one of the most beautiful women he had ever seen—bathing in the balmy night breezes. As she bathed herself so late at night, it would seem that the woman had no idea that she was being observed by Israel's king. Nor did she realize what was soon about to transpire. David, who did not yet know her name, made a decision that set him on a different course than the one God had planned for him. He determined to have this woman, no matter what it took to achieve it.

The king immediately sent a messenger to discover her identity. The godly man whose songs told of his passionate love for God should have known to drop everything right there when the messenger returned with news that this woman's name was Bathsheba—wife of Uriah, one of the bravest soldiers in the whole of King David's army. The most famous man in Israel was about to force his way into this woman's life, take what he wanted from it, and turn it upside down.

Bathsheba, whose husband was away fighting Israel's battles, heard a knock at the door. A messenger from the king! What could the king be thinking of, requesting her presence immediately! Yet her heart raced as she rushed past the palace guards at the messenger's heels, following him into the presence of the legendary king. Perhaps at that moment, her mind was filled with awe at the idea of actually meeting this great man. Was she preparing a list of questions she would like to ask this "man after God's own heart?" She, like all the people of Israel, was well aware of the many songs produced from the lips of this "Sweet Psalmist of Israel." She had heard them sung again and again. She knew the tales of valor extolling this shepherd boy who killed a lion and a bear, then a giant, led his armies into battle, and whose acts of courage had given back to Israel her sense of pride.

But David had other things on his mind that evening as the beautiful Bathsheba approached his throne. He soon made clear to her his intentions for a night they were to regret for the rest of their lives. Ripples of their night together would rock the nation and nearly wrench the kingdom from David's grasp. It would rend his family, change his future, and bring great heartache to both David and Bathsheba.

All this would happen to the man who had once penned the words, "As the deer pants for the water brooks, so pants my soul for You, O God" (Ps. 42:1) and "The Lord is my shepherd; I shall not want" (Ps. 23:1). He had loved God in a dear and tender way; yet even today he is remembered not only for his great victories, but also for his greatest defeat.

If you were to ask the average person, "What do you remember best about King David from the Bible?" their answer would probably be evenly divided between his felling of Goliath and his falling into adultery with Bathsheba. Goliath . . . and Bathsheba.

These two people represent his greatest victory and his greatest defeat. How long had Satan been preparing the snare of adultery to bring down David, who had proven so mighty in battle? Satan couldn't bring him down on the battlefield, so he brought him down in the bedroom.

A Lifetime of Regret

The story of David and Bathsheba does not end in physical death, as was the fate of that great man of strength, Samson—a man also known for his unbridled passions. They lived long enough to experience a lifetime of regret over what they had done—particularly King David, who had been given every blessing and advantage by the God he loved. Although David repented of his sin, his life seemed to never again reach the heights and pinnacles of his former walk with God.

And unlike Delilah, who the Bible portrays as a temptress who intentionally set out to ensnare Samson, Bathsheba is not portrayed as villainous. We do not read in Scripture that she set out to trap David. In actuality, King David's first trap seemed to be this: being in the wrong place, at the wrong time, then setting his eyes on the wrong things. He worked himself into the position of committing adultery almost single-handedly. All it took was *just one look!*

While Bathsheba certainly shared responsibility for the sin of adultery with the wayward king, she does not appear to be the primary culprit in this famous Bible story. How could King David, who had been such a spiritual giant, stoop so low that he plotted to draw another man's wife into the sin of adultery? For a few moments of pleasure, he experienced a lifetime of sorrow.

Anatomy of a Fall

How did it happen? Let's take a look at the circumstances surrounding David's fall. At the time it happened, David had known twenty years of prosperity and success. He was loved and honored by the people of Israel. He had won each war he fought. You might even say he was on a roll. Everything was going his way. What went wrong?

It started with a look.

1. He looked with longing at another man's wife. Sadly, he let it go much farther than that. Jesus said, "You have heard that it was said to those of old, 'You shall not commit adultery.' But I say to you that whoever looks at a woman to lust for her has already committed adultery with her in his heart" (Matt. 5:27, 28). The original Greek word Jesus used for the word *looked* in that passage of text refers to a "continuous act of looking." In other words, this was no ordinary incidental, involuntary glance. David's gazing upon Bathsheba was intentional and prolonged.

Today's world is filled with images that one can't help but see. We are constantly bombarded with seductive images that we have no control over—a picture on a billboard, a commercial on TV, even a person who walks across our path. But there is a difference between simply seeing something and saying, "I really wish I hadn't seen that, so I will not continue to look at it" and placing ourselves in the position of knowing that we will be intentionally exposed to things that will arouse us sensually.

We have heard it said, "Sow a thought, reap an act. Sow an act, reap a habit. Sow a habit, reap a character. Sow a character, reap a destiny." This is good advice today.

Job of the Old Testament knew his own propensity for sin. Therefore, he decided to make this solemn vow: "I have made a covenant with my eyes; why then should I look upon a young woman? . . . If my step has turned from the way, or my heart walked after my eyes . . . then let me sow, and another eat; yes, let my harvest be rooted out" (Job 31:1, 7–8).

Had David heeded Job's advice, he would have saved himself much grief. Instead, he looked at Bathsheba as she bathed nearby—and he kept on looking until he allowed lust for her to build within his heart. He could have repented then and there, then kept himself from returning to the rooftop for these late-night walks. But David didn't stop there.

2. Next, he inquired. He sent a messenger to discover the woman's identity. When he was told that she was Bathsheba, the wife of Uriah, that information should have stopped him dead in his tracks. But it did not. For that matter, he should never have inquired to start with—after all, he was a married man. But David had already taken the hook. Sin had drawn him all the way into its snare. He who had once said, "I will behave wisely in a perfect way. . . . I will set nothing wicked before my eyes; I hate the work of those who fall away" (Ps. 101:2–3) was now himself falling away.

Have you ever noticed that God doesn't make it easy to sin? There is a line drawn, and crossing it is not easy. God puts obstacles in the way. Perhaps it will be a Bible verse that you discover during your morning devotions. It will seem to leap out at you, convicting you not to do that thing the devil is currently trying to tempt you into doing. Perhaps you will hear a message at church that tugs at the strings of your heart: "Don't sin!" A Christian friend may cross your path and, in the course of conversation, bring up the exact thing you seem to be struggling with. The Holy Spirit will send clear warnings. He is trying to alert you: *danger ahead!*

Then, if you persist in going forward, *watch out*. Watch out for thinking, "This doesn't apply to me. I'm different. I can handle it."

It appears that David thought he could handle it when he inquired of Bathsheba's identity, then ordered her to be brought into his presence. Once he had her in his royal chambers, he had sexual relations with her. But when he discovered soon after that she had become pregnant, he still had time to come to his senses and put on the brakes. He could have said, "That's it! I've sinned. I'm going to confess it before God." Instead, he tried to cover it.

3. *He launched a cover-up*. Realizing that Bathsheba's husband was one of his best fighting men, David launched an elaborate cover-up that involved even more deception. He devised a scheme that would make the child appear to be Uriah's—not his. Telling his chief commander, Joab, to send Uriah home from battle, David intended to make it appear that his purpose was to honor this great soldier. When loyal Uriah returned home, it was to David's praise: "Uriah, you have been such a brave and valiant soldier. I'm so proud of you. I wanted to bring you home so you could spend the night with your wife. So go home and have a great time." Get it?

Uriah was so loyal to the king and his fellow soldiers that instead of sleeping at home with his wife, he spent the night outside, as he knew his fellows were doing on the battlefield far away. When David asked why he hadn't spent the night with

Bathsheba, Uriah replied, "I couldn't bear to think of the other soldiers out there on the battlefield, fighting for you, the king. I couldn't give myself such a luxury, so I slept outside."

Obviously, the Lord had placed an obstacle in David's path. By now, he should have said, "What am I doing? I've got to snap out of this! God, please forgive me!" Instead, he persisted. He launched yet another deception against Uriah. The next night, the king got him drunk before sending him to Bathsheba. To David's utter amazement, Uriah again spent the night outside.

Finally the king was desperate. He resorted to a truly heinous plan. Calling Joab, he ordered him to return to the battlefield and to send Uriah out into the thickest of the fighting, then withdraw, leaving him alone—outnumbered against the enemy—to defend himself. In other words, David was saying, "Make sure Uriah is killed." What is that sin called? Murder. Uriah's virtues had become violations in David's mind. The loyal soldier had thwarted his plans for a cover-up. Sure enough, when Joab and his men fell back from the fighting, it made Uriah a sitting-duck target. He was quickly cut down, fighting for his God, his king, and his country.

When King David heard of Uriah's death, he thought he had covered up his sin quite nicely. He instantly took Bathsheba as his wife and everything seemed to be working out fine. But David soon learned the truth of Proverbs 28:13: "He who covers his sins will not prosper. . . ." Although David appeared to have all his ducks in a row outwardly, he had forgotten one small thing. He had "displeased the Lord" (2 Sam. 11:27). The Bible says sin will find a person out (see Num. 32:23). God always has the last word.

4. David became incapacitated by guilt. It had not been a good year for David. To the casual observer, it may have seemed like business as usual, but David's unconfessed sin had begun to fester. Deep within his heart, that sin worked its way out in obscure ways. Gone was the joy that had marked him since childhood. In its place was a deadness of heart and a heaviness that grew hard as the stone walls he now hid behind.

Sin is tricky. David knew he had somehow pulled it off so he could marry the formerly married—now widowed—Bathsheba. But in his heart he knew that in order for it to happen, he had heaped sin upon sin. In his heart, he knew better than to do even one of the things that now kept him from fellowshiping with his God.

Some people today seem to have no remorse whatsoever over living a lifestyle of habitual sin that is displeasing to God. They seem to have no pangs of conscience, and appear to be handling everything just fine. Yet I have a hard time believing that any of these people could possibly do what they're doing and have a relationship with God.

When you don't know God, sin doesn't necessarily bother you. The fact that you can sin and not be bothered by it is a good indication that you don't know God. Why? The Bible says that if you do not experience God's chastening, or discipline, then you are not really His child (see Heb. 12:8). The greatest proof that you belong to God is not merely the joy that comes from walking with Him, but also the conviction that comes when you step out of line. When you truly know the Lord, you will not be happy living in sin. You will experience great turmoil. You will agonize over guilt. So if you are doing something that is displeasing to the Lord and you are now struggling with guilt and anguish, rejoice! It's an indication that you are His child, and also an indication that you need to repent.

David experienced a miserable year of guilt and unconfessed sin. He writes of that year: "When I kept silent, my bones wasted away through my groaning all day long. For day and night Your hand was heavy upon me; my strength was sapped as in the heat of summer" (Ps. 32:3–4, NIV).

Although David was miserable living in sin, he still refused to speak of it—to God or anyone. It took a prophet to expose it and to bring David back to reality. One day the prophet Nathan came to visit David in his royal chamber. David listened intently as the prophet described a situation. "There is a man who has a little pet lamb. In fact, his children love this lamb. They care so much for it. But this poor man has a neighbor who is rich and has many sheep. One day this man's rich neighbor received a visitor. He wanted to serve his guest a dinner of lamb. Instead of killing one of his own sheep, he took his neighbor's only pet lamb. Then he slaughtered it and served it to his guest. What should be done to such a man?" David's blood boiled as he listened to the injustice contained in Nathan's story. "This man should be put to death!" he asserted.

Now, doesn't that punishment seem to be a little extreme? I mean, it's bad to steal someone's lamb, but does lamb-theft really warrant the death penalty? Why not give the man who had been wronged one of the neighbor's many lambs in exchange? Give him four lambs. Give him a dozen. But kill him? David's response reveals how darkened were his thinking processes. He was not thinking rationally—had not been thinking rationally for some time, no doubt. He was not thinking justly. He was reacting from his passions—the passions that drove him away from God and into sin.

Funny how ugly sin looks when it is someone else who has committed it. Isn't it interesting that Jesus said, "Why do you look at the speck in your brother's eye, but do not consider the plank in your own eye?" (Matt. 7:3). The word Jesus used for "speck" and "plank" are one and the same in the Greek, implying that the two are of the same substance but that one is larger than the other. Jesus was saying that often a person will be quick to notice a modified version of the sin he himself is struggling with, failing to see how much that sin has truly taken over his own life.

Show me a person who is hyper-critical, and I will show you a person who is guilty of far worse sin in his own life. David was guilty of adultery and of premeditated murder. Yet he thought it perfectly just to kill a man who had merely stolen his neighbor's sheep. Of all people, King David should have been "Mr. Compassion." But instead, he was "Mr. Hypocrisy." He fell neatly into Nathan's little prophetic trap, as the prophet pointed his finger straight at David and said, *"You* are the man."

The hammer had finally dropped.

David's heart sank.

In a single moment, the charade had ended. David's plots came crashing down around him. He had been found out. The plank in his own eye had become acutely visible as David now realized the parallel the prophet had so expertly drawn. He was like the man who had so many sheep. And, like that man, he had stolen Uriah's wife—his only sheep—for himself. Yes, he was the guilty party.

5. *David repented*. Now that Nathan had broken through David's wall of resistance, the king quickly broke before the Lord. He repented tearfully. The prophet said, "All right. Your sin has been put away from you." Then he added something else. "Therefore, the sword will never depart from your house . . ." (2 Sam. 12:10, NIV). David, who had just been forgiven, was being told that he would also reap what he had sown.

Now you may be thinking, "He was forgiven—right?"

Right.

And you may be thinking, "And when God forgives, He also forgets. Right?"

Right.

You may even be thinking, "So if I go out tomorrow and sin, then repent, and ask God to forgive me, He'll do it. Right?"

Right.

Then you may be thinking, "So no problem. Right?"

Not exactly. The Bible does say that God will forgive us when we repent, turn away from sin, and turn back to Him. But nowhere does it say that we will necessarily escape all of sin's consequences.

For instance, you can rob a store, but if caught you will also be arrested for it. Let's say you're arrested for the crime and as the handcuffs are applied, you suddenly see the light. You turn to God and say, "I'm so sorry! Please forgive me!" If you have truly repented, I am confident that God will indeed forgive you. But I also am confident that you will probably do some jail time for robbery. The day you are scheduled to appear in court, it's doubtful that the judge will want to hear, "I know I was wrong, but I have asked God to forgive me." You will still be required to face the consequences and pay your debt to society.

David sinned. He asked for God's forgiveness, and he received it. But he also reaped the consequences of his sin. David saw the very sins he had committed reflected in the behavior of his children. One day his son, Amnon, began to burn with lust for his half-sister, Tamar. He tricked her into his presence by pretending to be sick and asking her to bake him a cake and serve it to him on his sickbed. When Amnon was alone with Tamar, he raped her. In essence, Amnon had treated Tamar as David had treated Bathsheba, only more violently. Later, when Tamar's brother, Absalom, heard what Amnon had done, he had Amnon killed. So Absalom treated Amnon as David had treated Uriah.

Tragically, David continued to reap the effects of his sin in his own household long after he had repented of his sin. In Proverbs 6:32, God warns us of the deadly implications of this sin called adultery: "A man who commits adultery lacks judgment; whoever does so destroys himself" (NIV).

David's life seems to parallel James 1:14 and 15: "Each one is tempted when he is drawn away by his own desires and enticed. Then, when desire has conceived, it gives birth to sin; and sin, when it is full grown, brings forth death."

Six Reasons to Avoid the Compromise of Adultery

If the story of King David does not convince you of how devastating the compromise of adultery actually is, here are six powerful reasons to avoid it.

1. You damage your spouse. The Bible teaches that when you have sexual relations with someone, a unique union takes place. You become "one" with this person. You may say it's just a "one-night fling," but the truth is, you have just become one with someone other than your spouse, thus dishonoring and damaging that special oneness that was previously only shared by the two of you.

Incidentally, adultery is the only sin for which Jesus gave a "release clause" in marriage. That's not to say that you should instantly get a divorce if there has been adultery in your marriage. No marriage should be automatically dissolved without the two parties attempting to do everything possible to work things out. Yet when one spouse commits adultery, the other spouse is damaged. Adultery inflicts great emotional pain on the spouse who has remained faithful. In many cases, the most devastating blow to your spouse is not so much the act of adultery—as painful as that may be—as the prolonged period of time you spend trying to cover your tracks.

I once heard about a man who had been unfaithful to his wife for seven years. She was devastated when she realized that he had been living a lie all that time. She felt betrayed as she thought of all the Christmases, children's birthdays, and anniversaries that they had celebrated during those seven years—while he was secretly unfaithful. What deception!

2. *You damage yourself.* A person who commits this sin must be in a backslidden state in order to do it. This person has probably been rationalizing for so long, they have forgotten which way is "up." The enemy will undoubtedly continue to try to attack this person in this area—even after they have returned to the Lord—because they crossed the line to begin with. Radical measures must be taken if this person is to keep from falling into this snare again. It's much easier to commit adultery the second time than it is the first.

Has it happened to you? If you think you should simply terminate your marriage and marry the person you have become involved with, *think again.* You are about to attempt to build a marriage on a very shaky foundation. In fact, you are about to build on sinking sand. Not only is what you are about to do both unbiblical and sinful, but how will you ever fully trust that person once you marry them? The whole relationship has been built on deception and mistrust. So will it be with the marriage. Statistics show that second marriages are twice as likely to fail as first ones. Third marriages fail even more frequently than second ones. The odds that marriage will end in divorce only go up with each new divorce and remarriage.

3. *You damage your children.* Please let me underscore this reason. If you are a man, your position as spiritual leader in the home is determined by your own hand. Not only does it erode the trust of your spouse when you commit adultery, but it also diminishes your children's ability to trust you. To make matters worse—as in the case of King David—your children may even repeat your sin.

I once heard about a teenage girl who had become sexually involved before marriage. Her parents sat her down and said, "Honey, we taught you not to do that. Why did you do it?" She replied, "Well, Dad did it." And she was right. Her dad had become involved in an adulterous relationship. What kind of example had he set? In that sense, he had made it easier for his daughter to follow in the footprints of his own sexual sin.

In today's society, men are not alone in the commission of this sin. Sadly, some women also fall into its snare. It is equally damaging for sons and daughters to lose their trust and confidence in their mother. Moms—think about the consequences before you compromise. The consequences last a lifetime.

4. *You damage the church.* Scripture teaches that in the church, when one of us suffers, we all suffer. When one member is exalted, we are all exalted. For instance, take a man like Billy Graham. When God works through him and when we see him offering a prayer for our nation at a presidential inauguration or some other well-publicized national event, Christians everywhere are blessed because he is our representative. We feel honored as he stands up for truth.

On the other hand, when a Christian leader falls, we feel the blow. We may have never met the person. Because he claims to follow Christ and has been lifted up to leadership within the church, we also take a hit when he falls. If was for this very reason that Paul exhorted the believers in Corinth to remove immoral men from their midst, saying, "A little leaven leavens the whole lump" (1 Cor. 5:6). Those who have not yet committed adultery are weakened by their very exposure to those who have. When the compromise of adultery occurs, the whole body of Christ suffers for it.

5. *You damage your witness, as well as the cause of Christ.* I only need to cite the examples of several well-known televangelists to make this point. To me, the term "televangelist" is a media created term that has nothing to do with the God-given office and calling of an evangelist. An evangelist is someone who primarily proclaims the message of the gospel. In my opinion, many of these televangelists were not evangelists at all. In fact, in a recent reader poll, *Christianity Today* learned that the number one reason more people today do not share their faith is because of these embarrassing scandals. To me, that sounds like a convenient excuse. But it just goes to show you how much damage one person falling into the snare of adultery can cause. Not only is their own witness for Christ damaged—often irreparably—but so is the cause of Christ damaged.

Perhaps you have told your friends in the workplace, "I'm a Christian." You may have a bumper sticker on your car emblazoned with some Christian slogan. You bring your Bible to work. Then one day your mostly non-believing co-workers discover that you have been stepping out on your spouse. Now they have a very convenient peg to hang their doubts on. You begin to overhear the whispers at the drinking fountain, around the copier, and in the hallway. You know you've got it coming, but it still hurts.

When you fall into this sin, you lose your integrity and ruin your witness. After Nathan pointed out David's sin to him, he said, "By this deed you have given great occasion to the enemies of the Lord to blaspheme . . . " (2 Sam. 12:14). Likewise, in falling into this snare, you will give ammunition to the enemy to use against the Church.

6. *You sin against the Lord.* This should be the primary reason to avoid the sin of adultery, but sadly, it is probably the last thing some people even stop to consider. The young man, Joseph, kept this in mind when he resisted the charms offered to him by Potiphar's wife. When she tried to sexually entrap him, he replied, "How then can I do this great wickedness, and sin against God?" (Gen. 39:9).

He had the right perspective. Our highest motive should always be to please God. Our great love for Him should be what keeps us from falling into the sin of adultery or any other trap or compromise, for that matter. One of the best definitions of *the fear of the Lord* that I have ever heard is "a wholesome dread of displeasing Him." Of all the deterrents I have mentioned, this one should be the strongest.

Pleasing God should be the primary thing that keeps us from adultery. Our love for God should bear the fruit of our hatred of sin. Remember—it was when David drifted away from his intimacy with God that he became vulnerable to sin's enticements.

Four Steps to Build Your Spiritual Resistance

There are steps you can take to build up your resistance in this area. Let's examine them, one step at a time.

Step 1: Walk with God. When you do this, you will be like Joseph. When the temptation to sin comes knocking, you will have at your disposal the same power, will, and spiritual resources to stand strong in the face of temptation. Develop, cultivate, and tend to your intimacy with God. Fellowship with Him is the greatest deterrent there is against sin.

Step 2: Walk with your spouse. Work to keep friendship, romance, and intimacy alive with your spouse. You may say, "Oh, but the romance left our marriage long ago!" Well, romance is not something that just mystically hovers around, even though that's how many people seem to envision it. No—it's something two people work to keep alive. If you want romance in your marriage, then take some practical steps to put it there. If the fire seems to be flickering down, throw another log on it!

Remember when you first began to court? Retrace some of those steps. Spend a quiet night over dinner in a nice restaurant. Tell your spouse how much you love him or her, how attractive they still are to you, how much you appreciate them. Remember when you first dated your spouse? You talked about everything. You shared your thoughts. You said, "I love you," often. You spent time together. Now ask, "Is it the same today?" If not, the romance has probably left your marriage.

Go after it! You can get it back. It's something that you work to keep alive. Pick up the phone and call your spouse for no other reason than to say, "I'm thinking about you. I appreciate you. You're wonderful. I love you!" Communicate. Keep the friendship going. Just as we commune with God, we must also commune with each other.

Step 3: Don't walk in the counsel of the ungodly. Psalm 1 contains some very good advice. It tells us, "Blessed (or happy) is the man who walks not in the counsel of the ungodly, nor stands in the way of sinners, nor sits in the seat of the scornful." Avoid flirtatious friendships and overly close relationships with the opposite sex at all costs. You may think I'm a bit legalistic for saying this, but I think if married we should seriously reconsider having close friendships with someone of the opposite sex who is not our spouse.

Most affairs do not begin with sex but with friendship. Intimacy begins to develop as the "friendship" progresses a step farther than it should have been allowed to progress. Both parties begin to bare their hearts. Soon they are revealing their deepest feelings. Then that "friendship" begins to evolve into something more.

You can't believe it's happening. How did you become entangled in this sticky web? You never intended it to go this far.

You expected to always honor the vows between you and your spouse, the vows you made on your wedding day.

This is how easy it is to become embroiled in something that could end in adultery.

Recognize this potential weakness—and avoid it. Let your spouse be your only best friend, and the only close and intimate friend you have of the opposite sex. Work to rekindle those fires of romance. It's good insurance against the compromise of adultery and, let's face it, it's pretty wonderful!

Step 4: Count the cost. Remember the price of adultery. It is staggering. It lasts a lifetime. Are you ready to face the shame when your sin goes public? Do you want to be marked as an embarrassment to the cause of Christ? Are you ready to lose your witness, the respect of your spouse, the trust of your children? Are you ready for the pain that your sin will inflict upon your family? Count the cost. You may reap the consequences for a lifetime for those few moments of guilty pleasure. Is it worth it?

Some Staggering Statistics

Adultery is devastating. At its worst, it will result in divorce and lifelong bitterness. It establishes walls within parent-child relationships that may never be taken down. At the very least, it undermines the bond of trust and love between a husband and wife. While it is possible for a marriage to recover from the devastation of adultery, it is a difficult road to recovery which often requires the innocent spouse to forgive the guilty one if trust is ever to be restored.

Just how widespread is adultery in our culture today? Studies reveal that 40 to 50 percent of all married men have had extramarital affairs. One survey pointed out that nearly 70 percent of all married men under forty *expect* to have an extramarital relationship. Imagine that! Seventy percent of one entire age group *expect to be unfaithful to their wives.* In essence, these men are *affairs waiting to happen.* Given the exceedingly permissive views of our society toward sex, researchers Gilbert Ness and Robert Libby have predicted that between one-half and two-thirds of all husbands will have had an affair before they reach forty.

But the men are not alone in this "new morality." The women are quickly catching up. Because more women are now out in the marketplace with full-time careers, they are closing the ranks. In 1953, one-half of married men had been unfaithful to their wives, yet only 26 percent of wives could respond in kind. Today's studies reveal that 41 percent of married women openly admit they've cheated on their husbands.

Oprah Winfrey conducted a survey among her television audience regarding the movie, *Indecent Proposal,* in which a character played by Robert Redford offers to pay the character played by Demi Moore a million dollars just for sleeping with him for one night. A million bucks would settle her husband's staggering gambling debt. It would pay off their delinquent mortgage. When Oprah asked her studio audience, "If you were offered a million dollars to sleep with a man, would you do it?" 55 percent said "yes."

What a telling picture of today's society. It's been said that men give love to get sex and women give sex to get love. Women want to be loved. They want security. They want to feel safe, appreciated. Many young girls and boys repeat the patterns of sexual sin they witnessed being committed by their parents in their own homes. They haven't got a clue that what they're doing is sinful in God's eyes. They are simply replaying the sin that has been visited down from one generation to the next. One-fifth of the nation's children will lose their virginity by the age of thirteen. Seventy percent of high school students say they had sex by graduation time. Instead of "trickle-down economics," we are witnessing "trickle-down immorality." Unless we do something to establish a biblical moral code in our own homes, we're doomed to let society dictate morality—or the lack of it— to our children.

You may say, "Well, Greg, I know it's bad. But these are things that are happening within secular society. It's not that bad in the church." Want to bet? I must disagree.

In a random sampling of a thousand subscribers, *Christianity Today* learned that 45 percent of the respondents admitted to having committed adultery or acting inappropriately regarding sexual matters.

Billy Graham has called immorality an epidemic in our churches as well as the secular world at large. He has cited a poll claiming that 40 percent of the young people in Bible-believing evangelical churches are sexually active. The poll also revealed that 60 percent of single adults, including those who attend church regularly and participate in Bible studies, are not only sexually active, but half report having sex with multiple partners. No wonder the world is in such a state of turmoil. For that matter, no wonder the church is not having much of an impact on the world.

What to do When it Seems too Late

Have you already crossed that line? Are you committing adultery? Are you planning on it? Have you been thinking about it? If your answer is "yes," I urge you to repent. Turn to God and ask His forgiveness. Stop now. "Thou shalt not commit adultery" is one of the Ten Commandments. It is one of the ten sins God views as most serious of all.

First Corinthians 6:9 says, "Do you not know that the wicked will not inherit the kingdom of God? Do not be deceived: Neither the sexually immoral nor idolaters nor adulterers . . . nor homosexual offenders . . . will inherit the kingdom of God" (NIV).

Don't spend another day in that "go nowhere" extra-marital relationship. Turn to the Lord and He will help you to work things out with your spouse and your family. He will help you through the guilt and anguish. Thank God, He is a forgiving God. Thank God, He is faithful to restore. While you cannot expect to go back to things exactly as before, you can believe God to restore the love, faith, and trust you and your spouse once shared. Your marriage has taken a difficult hit. But thank God, He is a God who can put it back together. If you are not married, stay sexually pure! Don't sacrifice your virginity, for it cannot be regained. Forgiven—yes. Regained? Sadly, no.

An intense love for God and for your spouse will see you through this difficult time. Stop looking for loopholes. The Lord will guide you safely through the rough waters of sexual temptation. I don't have some magic formula I can give you that will make it so that you will never be tempted again. It's a daily battle. But I can tell you this—once you begin to lower your guard again in this area, you will become a target once more.

If you are providing target practice for the enemy's fiery darts called "adultery," face it. It's time to move forward again with God. It's harder to hit a moving target than a stationary one. Those who are moving forward with Christ, those who are growing in their love for Him and working to keep the fires of romance burning within their marriages, are not nearly as easy for the devil to hit as those who have grown stagnant and bored in their marriages. Those who have let their guards down can easily become be the next victims of adultery's flaming arrows. Keep moving forward, and God will strengthen both your marriage and your resolve.

LET'S PRAY

If you are currently caught in the snare of adultery, why don't you make a recommitment to God right now?

Father, please forgive me. I have committed the sin of adultery. I cry out to You for forgiveness and ask You to wash me and make me clean. Cleanse me of this sin, for I repent of it. I ask You to help my spouse and my family to forgive me, and to bring us to the place of restoration. God, heal my marriage. Heal my spouse and my children of the pain I have caused them. Bring my relationship with You and with my family to a place of strength and safety. Restore romance, I pray, to my marriage and help me to serve You with fervor once again. In Jesus' name, I pray. Amen.

8

THE WILDFIRE OF IMMORALITY

Flee sexual immorality.

—1 Corinthians 6:18

California's wildfires are infamous. Once they start, they seem to be "unstoppable." When wildfire sweeps through a California community, it leaves behind a darkened swatch of burned stubble. Oddly, some homes and businesses are eerily spared from the fate of their charred neighbors. The flames occasionally stop and redirect themselves, leaving someone's home relatively unscathed—but burning their nearby neighbors' homes to the ground.

It reminds me of a story about a man who had this experience. Like his neighbors, he feared for the safety of his home and possessions. Unlike his neighbors, his home was spared from the flames. Feeling rather relaxed, as if life just might be back to normal again, he bundled up his clothes and took them to a nearby cleaning service. Since this man was single, he habitually waited until everything he owned needed cleaning before dropping his clothes off at the cleaners. This was one of those times. Down to his shorts and one suit, shirt, and tie, he planned to take his claim check to the cleaners the following day after work, and—presto! He and his wardrobe of expensive suits, designer shirts, and ties would be in business once more.

But before that could happen, another wildfire blew up—seemingly from nowhere. Overnight it leveled the neighborhood where his cleaners was located, wiping out everything in view for several city blocks. The clothes that had been spared the flames of wildfire near home had been consumed by the same wildfire that had simply moved to the other side of town.

There's something strange about wildfire. You can't trust it. Just when you think you've got it under control, it will turn on you and begin to move.

"Devil" Winds

In 1992 I was among those who watched anxiously as Southern California experienced one of the worst wildfires in its history. To blame were many small fires that had fueled one huge one, made even more vicious by what Californians call the Santa Anas—also known as "devil" winds. It was an amazing thing to watch. Just when the flames seemed to be confined to a particular area, within minutes the winds would pick the embers up and blow them in an entirely new direction—sometimes as far as several miles away. When the toll was finally taken, these firestorms had destroyed literally hundreds of homes and businesses in their path, leaving behind blackened, charred remains.

I will never forget opening up the newspaper after these devastating fires and seeing a photograph of an entire upscale neighborhood that had been wiped out overnight. The only thing left of these affluent homes were foundations and chimneys. Then my eye was drawn to an interesting sight. Right there in the midst of all this burned, charred, rubble stood one lone home—untouched. Not only had it been untouched by the flames, but it did not even appear to be damaged by smoke! This gleaming white house stood in stark contrast to the ruin all around it.

When this homeowner was asked why his home still stood while his neighbors' homes lay in ashes, he replied that he had simply gone the extra mile—way beyond city building codes—to make his home flame retardant. That included installing double-paned windows, thick stucco walls, sealed eaves, concrete tile, and abundant insulation. Firefighters said, "It was clear to us that this would be a place to make a stand." Because this man had taken extra fireproofing precautions, his house survived the flames when they actually hit.

In much the same way, Satan—the master arsonist—has caused massive devastation by fueling the fires of lust and passion. Homes are being leveled. Families are being displaced and destroyed. Our country is being ravaged by the wildfires of immorality. Unless we take the necessary precautions, we could be their next victims.

Nothing to Toy With

When I was a kid, I used to love to burn my plastic army men. As I held each little green plastic guy above a match, I would gleefully watch as he curled up, then melted down. Why I derived so much enjoyment from something as strange as this, I don't yet understand. I thought it was great fun to watch these little toy soldiers turn into a hot puddle of burning plastic. Of course, I would always wait until my parents were away before attempting such a feat of "junior arson." When they were safely away, I would set my small army up on a piece of newspaper, take out a book of matches, and light them—one by one—then watch as they melted into oblivion.

One day I decided to raise the stakes. I lit three at once. This time, the flames melted the three little plastic men down into one giant puddle of goo—and caught the newspaper on fire too. Now I had a big blaze going. In another classic bad decision, I wadded the whole thing up and tossed it into a nearby waste basket. It was made of rattan—very flammable. It too caught fire. I could have burned the entire house down had I not gotten control of the fire. I learned a valuable lesson that day about the rapid spread of fire, and it cured me of my pyromaniac ways.

Toying with lust and immorality is a little more dangerous than trying to melt down little, green plastic soldiers. This type of compromise is much more flammable and can bring about permanent disaster. You may think, "I can handle this! No problem!" But suddenly the burning embers of lust begin to spark again, and suddenly fresh flames are blowing over your life. Now you find that you have lost complete control. You're about to get burned, but so will a lot of other people—people you love. What happened? About this age-old malady, the Bible says, "Can a man scoop fire into his lap without his clothes being burned" (Prov. 6:27, NIV)?

The answer, of course, is "no." Fire is too unpredictable.

Yet some people think they can handle it. That's what Samson thought as he toyed with the temptress, Delilah.

Samson and Delilah

In much the same way he brought down King David, the devil banked the fires of lust and desire within the great Old Testament judge and warrior, Samson. When ensnared by the charms of the temptress, Delilah, Samson succumbed in such a way that he was made completely vulnerable. Here was a man upon whom the power and strength of God rested. He had been able to vanquish many enemies in the name of the Lord Jehovah. He was able to resist temptation of many types . . . until it was presented to him in the form of the beautiful Delilah.

The name *Delilah* actually means "delicate." Her snares were lined with silk. Satan used this delicate "weapon" to launch a clever "sneak attack" against Israel's mightiest man—a man who had once killed a thousand Philistines with the jawbone of a donkey. Delilah was used as a tool by the enemy to discover the secret source of Samson's strength and take it from him. For many months she wooed him and began to break down his resolve, as she repeatedly attempted to learn from him the secret of his strength. Unknown to Samson, Delilah had made an agreement with the Philistines to exchange that secret for a great deal of wealth. Several times Samson lied and told her that his strength had to do with this, or that. He toyed with her until she caught onto his game of cat and mouse. Yet as he spent more and more time in her presence—thinking he could handle it, believing he was in total charge—he came closer to telling her the truth. Finally he could hold out no longer. As Delilah wrapped her arms about him, Samson lost all his resolve, and blurted out the truth. He told her that the secret of his strength was his committment to God which involved taking the vow of a Nazarite. And one of the requirements of that vow was to never cut his hair. When she persisted in her interrogation, he explained that God had instructed him not to cut his hair. His long hair was the key to his great physical prowess.

A little later, when he awoke from sleep, he discovered that his hair had been cut. Weak as a kitten, it was not difficult for the waiting Philistines to drag the now-tame Samson off in chains. They put out his eyes and put him to work as a slave, performing hard labor in a place where passersby could see the fate of this once-mighty, once-powerful individual who had done great exploits for God. He was mocked and shamed and had much time to repent before God and seek forgiveness for his sin.

Samson is another example of a man who fell out of fellowship with God because he could not—or would not—bridle his physical passions. Consequently, he fell victim to Delilah's schemes.

The biblical account of the story of Samson reveals that he did repent and cry out to the Lord. He pleaded for one last opportunity to be used as an instrument of God's vengeance against his captors. He received that opportunity when, during a public feast in honor of the Philistines' pagan god, his captors chained him between the pillars of the temple. Once more the power of God descended upon Samson, and once more he was used mightily to glorify God. The message? God hears the heart of the penitent, and He will restore them. But while Samson's spiritual condition was restored, his story ended in his physical death. As the stones of the temple rumbled and fell, scores of Philistines were crushed beneath the rubble—Samson too. That final feat of strength cost him his life, but not before sin had cost him everything.

A Deadly Snare

Lust can be an equally deadly snare. Perhaps it has led you into premarital sex. Perhaps, if you are married, it has led you into an adulterous affair. Whatever its form, the wildfire of immorality has swept across your life and is ruining it, as well as the lives of those you love. It is responsible for the ruined lives of many young people who—caught up in the fires of its passions—found they were HIV positive or afflicted with other serious, sexually transmitted diseases.

But let's say you're a loyal believer, faithful to your spouse. You say, "Wait a minute, Greg. I don't need to hear this. I would never fall into that type of sin. My spouse and I have an ideal marriage. I can't imagine any circumstance in which I would be unfaithful."

I heard something like that one day as a prominent author discussed on a Christian talk show the tragic consequences of his own adulterous affair. He, too, had once believed his marriage to be "ideal." This particular individual would even sometimes boast to his friends, "If I ever fall into sin, I guarantee it will not be adultery. Anything but that. I love my wife so much that it would never happen to me."

Ironically, the very sin this man said he would never commit was the sin he fell victim to a short while later. After a stormy period of failure, followed by repentance, restoration, and recovery, this man concluded: "An unguarded strength is a double weakness." I agree.

See how dangerous it is to believe we'll never fall into sin? Whenever someone boasts of something like this man did, I get the shivers. I know he—or she—is skating on very thin ice. As 1 Corinthians 10:12 states, "Let him who thinks he stands take heed lest he fall." Any of us at any time are capable of sinning. Let's not forget that very important fact.

The Bible says, "The heart is deceitful above all things, and desperately wicked" (Jer. 17:9). And Paul states, "I know that in me (that is, in my flesh) nothing good dwells" (Rom. 7:18). That verse does not mean that I will automatically go out and commit sin, unrestrained. It simply means the potential to sin is ALWAYS present, as long as I am in this physical body on earth.

Who Will Teach the Children?

In our increasingly value-free, "anything goes" society—a society that will not allow the Ten Commandments to be posted on the classroom walls, but will freely hand out condoms at school—the only way we can hope to infuse moral values back into society is through the teaching at home. A recent *USA Today* front-page story about the spread of crime in America stated, "Crime and the growing fear of it has muscled aside the economy to take control of the nation's political agenda and public mindset. People feel personally threatened by what they consider a complete collapse of the fabric of society," said Ethel Cline, a New York pollster and political consultant. When asked the question, "Which factors do you see as most important in causing crime?" 89 percent of the people polled replied, "A lack of moral training in the home."[1]

What is the answer to the growing epidemic of crime? Our police forces are understaffed. Our bureaucracy only contributes to the problems in many ways. Quite frankly, the only hope for our country may be the values children learn at home. It would seem that the cure for crime is not the electric chair, but the highchair. Establishing a godly foundation begins early. No wonder the devil has launched such a virulent attack against the home and family values.

Yet what is it that appears to be devastating more families than anything else today? Wildfire! Immorality! Sexual infidelity! If we are to instill proper Christian values in our children at home, it is imperative that we live them out in front of them on a daily basis. We must be keenly aware of these erosive forces bringing pressure to bear on every side—and fight them. If our homes are to stand the test of fire—as did the home of the man who had taken the right precautions—we, too, must take extra precautions to see that our families are "fireproofed" against the wildfire of immorality.

The Story of Balak and Balaam

Certainly sexual temptation has been around since the fall of man. But I think everyone will agree that at no time in biblical history has there been a time such as now, when sexual permissiveness is so unprecedented. Historians of the future will undoubtedly look back on this time and determine that ours was a civilization that was absolutely obsessed with sex.

Returning to the text we have been following since the beginning of *The Great Compromise,*—1 Corinthians, chapter 10—we read: "Nor let us commit sexual immorality, as some of them did, and in one day twenty-three thousand fell" (v. 8). This particular story that Paul is referring to is found in the Old Testament Book of Numbers. It's the story of the greedy prophet, Balaam. He was a paradoxical and unusual character, to say the least. You might say that he was a mercenary prophet, or a prophet for hire, except for the fact that he should have spelled his title "profit" instead of "prophet." The Bible portrays Balaam as a man who was more interested in "preying" than in "praying."

At the time this story took place, King Balak of the Moabites was seeking the key to defeating the Israelites. If he could just get the edge he was seeking, he would have all Israel in his clutches. He thought that perhaps the answer would be to find a prophet to curse the Israelites. Then he and his band of men would sweep down and recover the spoils. That would be much simpler than relying on superior strength on the battlefield, now wouldn't it?

Somehow, King Balak found the willing Balaam and with the promise of a lucrative payoff, Balaam happily complied. As he went about his work, trying to find a curse that would stick to the people of Israel, the Lord spoke to this misguided mercenary. He told him in no uncertain terms not to curse Israel but to bless them. Needless to say, this was not exactly the news that King Balak was hoping for.

Now greedy Balaam was in a real quandary. He could smell money, but he was under strict orders from God not to curse Israel. So he came up with a complicated plot to get Israel to bring a curse upon themselves. He devised a plan to lure the Israelite men into the company of Moabite women. As the men had sexual relations with these idol-worshiping women, the men became exposed to the idol-gods of the Moabites. Those who went into the tents to worship these idol-gods would bring down the wrath of God upon the people of Israel. Clever.

Balak loved it. He even took charge of enlisting the women to do his dirty work. The young men of Israel easily fell into this sensuous trap. The Bible says, "While Israel was staying in Shittim, the men began to indulge in sexual immorality with Moabite women, who invited them to the sacrifices to their gods. So Israel joined in worshiping the Baal of Peor. The people ate and bowed before these gods and the Lord's anger burned against them" (Num. 25:1–3, NIV). As a result, God's judgment came down. After all was said and done, 24,000 Israelites were dead, destroyed by the hand of God as it rested in judgment upon this sin of idol worship. But the real destructive force was immorality. The 24,000 Israelites were not the first people to be destroyed by immorality; nor will they be the last.

Paul's Warning to the Corinthians—and Us

Paul had two groups of people in mind when he wrote his warning to the church at Corinth in 1 Corinthians, chapter 10. He was addressing his warning to the people at Corinth, as well as to believers in the last days. That's us. Those Corinthian believers were a bit smug. They thought that somehow they were immune to sexual sin, since they were so knowledgeable spiritually. They had a blind spot, so to speak, when it came to immorality, idolatry, or other spiritual error. That's why Paul felt it imperative to warn them.

At the time of his letter to the Corinthians, sin was rampant in Corinth. In fact, idol worship was rampant. Towering above the ruins of old Corinth is a two-thousand-foot-high mountain fortress called Acrocorinth. In Paul's day, the Temple of Aphrodite sat atop that hill. Aphrodite, goddess of fertility, was one of the chief idols worshiped by the people of the day. In Aphrodite's temple, as many as a thousand prostitute priestesses would carry on their immoral activities, all in the name of worship, of course. History records that these prostitute priestesses would walk through the streets of Corinth, wearing specially designed sandals that left the words "Follow me" imprinted in the sand. Many citizens of Corinth did just that. They followed the priestesses to the high places, where their pagan temple was located, and they "worshiped" Aphrodite—an excuse to commit adultery, idolatry, and immorality.

Are we not hearing the same message—"Follow me"—today? It's everywhere. We see it on prime-time television, in programming touting the thrills and chills of unrestricted sex. We see it in the faces of emaciated models whose scantily clad bodies appear on the covers of major magazines, enticing young girls to look the same if they are to be thought of as appealing. "Follow me!" We see those words flashed yet again in the lyrics of rock music, as its listeners hear today's icons of pop, rap, and hip-hop hype a "make up your own rules you go along" rebellion mentality. "Follow me!"

Michael Medved, the social commentator and film historian, has pointed out, "An exhaustive study done by Louis Harris and Associates found that in the prime afternoon and evening hours, the three largest television networks broadcast a total of more than 65,000 sexual references every year. The study determined that the average American TV viewer now views 14,000 references to sex in the course of a year. One person said, 'Prime time implies that there is no fun without sin and no kiss unless it is a stolen one.'"[2] In other words, the presentation of sex on television is never within the context of marriage. It is almost always portrayed as something that occurs outside marriage, if it is to be exciting.

One expert gave a sad commentary of our society when he noted, "The new American hearth—the center for family activities, conversation, and companionship—is the TV." Think about how many families today sit behind TV trays, mesmerized by the images flickering from the television set, instead of sitting around a table, enjoying a leisurely evening meal followed by stimulating conversation. Now no one talks. They listen to an endless drone of televised messages, many of which are nonverbal, subliminal, and highly erosive. With this constant bombardment against the senses going on around us every day, we must consciously work to keep our guard up.

The Bible tells us, "The body is not meant for sexual immorality, but for the Lord, and the Lord for the body . . . Do you not know that your bodies are members of Christ himself? Shall I then take the members of Christ and unite them with a prostitute? Never! Do you not know that he who unites himself with a prostitute is one with her in body? For it is said, 'The two will become one flesh. . . . Flee from sexual immorality" (1 Cor. 6:13, 15–18).

God warns us about sexual immorality for our own good. There is really no such thing as a "one-night fling." The results of such an act often go on forever. When we cross that line of protection that God has placed around us, we do so at our own peril. The repercussions can go on for months, years—even a lifetime.

"But," you say, "I couldn't help it. I just fell into it." Come on—we both know that just isn't true. You knew for weeks, maybe even months ahead of time, that this was bound to happen. Before you ever actually acted anything out, you allowed your mind to become polluted with all sorts of fantasies, imaginations, and impure thoughts. After awhile those were no longer satisfying. That's really when you crossed the line. You began to flirt and spend more time with the object of your secret affections. But soon that didn't satisfy you either. So you stepped things up a bit. Soon you and the other party were having long, soul-baring conversations. That's what really led to immorality—

a chain of things that you could have stopped at any juncture before they got out of hand. It's not that you started out saying, "I'm going to act in an immoral manner and thereby destroy my home, hurt my kids, devastate my wife, break up my marriage, and reduce my Christian witness." No. Instead, you said, "We're just friends. There isn't anything to it. I'm just sharing. I can stop . . . any time I want."

Watch out! You're about to be singed by the wildfire of immorality.

Fear Always Follows

Say you've crossed the line. Now you've got to keep everything hidden. Under wraps. Secret. But deep down you fear the phone call that will be coming any day now—the one in which you are confronted with your secret sin. Guilt nags at your guts month after month. Then years. That's what the Bible says will happen when you commit this miserable, devastating sin—the sin of immorality that is slowly and surely destroying our culture from within.

It's time to draw a new line, then defend it. I know this isn't a pleasant message, but it's a needed one. It's vital that we confront this important area of compromise and deal with it head up. Straight on. Face to face. We must overcome immorality, or it will overcome us.

To overcome it, we must equip ourselves with fireproof armor that will deflect the arrows of the enemy when those arrows come, because—trust me—they will come.

LET'S PRAY

If you have been singed by the wildfires of immorality, will you pray and turn from it?

Father, please forgive me. I came too close to the wildfires of immorality. I have been burned, and others have been hurt as well by this sin that I've been caught up in. Please cleanse me now, as I repent before You.

Bring restoration to my life and the lives of the loved ones I have hurt. Please heal us and help us through this difficult time.

I turn to You, Father, to help me "fireproof" my life against the constant bombardment of immoral choices and images. Help me, Lord, to make the right choices, based on Your Word, then stand by them. In Jesus' name, I pray. Amen.

PART 3

THE FIGHT
AGAINST COMPROMISE

9

WARNING! NOW ENTERING
THE SPIRITUAL WAR ZONE!

For the weapons of our warfare are not carnal but mighty in God for pulling down strongholds.

—*2 Corinthians 10:4*

The troops had been building up for days. First, a line of blue, then a line of grey poured into the flat ground lying low between an outcropping of hills at the foot of the Blue Ridge mountains. There was bound to be bloodshed. But no one knew how much blood was about to be spilled on the green Pennsylvania hills of Gettysburg.

Thousands of soldiers glutted the farmlands and pastures, waiting for dawn and orders to move. The men knew that who would die and who would live was completely in God's hands, as was who would be the victors. The night before the fighting, harmonica music floated pleasantly on the balmy spring air. Fires from both Yankee and Confederate camps flickered like hundreds of small, delicate fireflies, dotting the hillsides with strange beauty. A battle was about to rage. More than seven thousand men were about to meet their Maker. But on this night—the night before the war cries were heard—General Ullysses S. Grant's men were clotted around a campfire, whispering their strategies to one another, acknowledging their secret fears.

It appears that Grant's men were impressed by—even afraid of—the South's Commander-in-Chief, General Robert E. "Bobby" Lee. Whenever they whispered his name, they did so reverently. "He's a brilliant strategist," one crusty old sergeant admitted. "You never quite know how he's going to move," another officer observed. "Wish we had 'im on *our* side," one Yankee old-timer said wistfully.

Wounds still run deep in the Pennsylvania hills near Gettysburg. Battles waged there between Union and Confederate armies were most costly. The dead, wounded, missing, or captured numbered forty-five thousand. Those who live near Gettysburg still seem to sense that the land remains blood-soaked from that historic Civil War battle. In fact, some of the blood spilled there still marks stones that survived the most famous battle of the Civil War—the one that placed victory squarely into Union hands. Ironically, the blood stains are still red—nearly a hundred and thirty years later.

Just as the North and South chose sides and divided up to fight a war that would determine whether or not the United States remained unified, so have Christians and the devil and his demonic forces chosen sides and divided up to fight the fight of faith.

In his book, *The Civil War,* author Geoffrey C. Ward tells a story about a scene that took place on a battlefield during the Gettysburg fighting. I use it to illustrate the type of attitude we Christians should have toward our adversary, the devil:

> Right in the middle of the Battle of the Wilderness, all the staff men who'd been fighting in the East all this time—Grant had just come from the West—kept talking, "Bobby Lee, Bobby Lee, he'll do this, that, and the other." And Grant finally told them, "I'm tired of hearing about Bobby Lee. You'd think he was going to do a double somersault and land in our rear. Quit thinking about what he's going to do to you and think about what you're going to do to him."[1]

What Are You Going to Do to the Devil?

Have you ever encountered a believer who was paralyzed by fear? I have—lots of times. This type of believer spends a lot of time telling you how powerful the devil is—how he roams about like a raging lion, lurking around waiting to pounce on Christians . . . how he makes his presence known in every type of worldly thing, polluting the whole environment for Christians who are just trying to serve God and live holy. By the time they're finished telling you how active the devil is, they have also admitted how scared they are of him. He has just received glory—instead of God, who is mightier, more powerful, and well able to keep us from the evil one.

I'm not saying the devil isn't powerful. We have already covered that issue. What I am saying is that we are in a war against him, and if we are to win it, it is vital that we fight from the position of victory. We are already the victors. That's what the Bible says.

Yet why is it that as believers, we often become so preoccupied with what the devil is doing that we also become paralyzed by fear? At times each of us may find ourselves overwhelmed by the well-oiled machinery of hell. Its influence seems to be spreading by the minute. Every minute, violent crimes are being committed—the likes of which have never been seen at any other time in history. During the past three decades, violent crime has increased 560 percent. Illegitimate births have increased 400 percent. Divorce rates have quadrupled. The rate of children being raised in single-parent households has tripled, as has the teen suicide rate. Every year, in the U.S. alone, 23,000 citizens are murdered. Six million other violent crimes are committed in the U.S. annually. According to the FBI, the number of violent crimes reported to police jumped from 168 per 100,000 people in 1963 to 758 per 100,000 people today. Today's crimes—crimes like drive-by shootings, crack wars, gang-banging, car-jackings, and parent-killing—were virtually unheard of a generation ago. Now these terms are part of America's new vocabulary.

When we look at these things, instead of keeping our eyes on God, it's no wonder we find it so difficult to walk in victory. It's very difficult not to be moved by what we see around us when we take a good look at the strangle-hold the devil has on national and world politics, as well as the entertainment industry. It may even seem that the devil has the upper hand. If we aren't careful, we'll become like those Union soldiers who had magnified their enemy into an almost super-human force to contend with.

Have You Read the End of the Book?

As I have already pointed out, although the devil has considerable power, he also has clear limitations. For that reason, we need to think about making him wonder what our next move is going to be, spiritually speaking, rather than spending time worrying about what he's going to do next.

Have you read the end of the Book? *We win!* That's right—the Book of Revelation assures believers of the victory, as Jesus Christ returns for His church and locks the devil and his henchmen up for a thousand years of peace on earth. But wait! There's more! As if a thousand years of peace were not enough victory, the Bible says that at the end of the thousand years, there will be another brief season of confrontation with a temporarily loosed devil. But again he will be defeated—this time *forever!* Banished forever to a continuously burning lake of fire, the devil will one day have no ability whatsoever to exert his evil influence on believers.

He knows that. That's why he is so active on the earth today. He knows his time is limited and that it will one day end—forever.

To me, this type of assurance is pretty encouraging. It even makes me feel brave to know that my Commander-in-Chief, Jesus, was, is, and will always be more powerful than the devil. While the devil can't be everywhere at once, Jesus can. As we seek His wisdom and leadership in this spiritual battle we are in, our Commander Jesus will give us insight into the strategies of the devil, exposing those plans and ruining their effectiveness.

In any military battle, there is great advantage gained when one can anticipate the enemy's next move. We should not be intimidated by the devil and his demon forces, because God has shown us in His Word how to effectively counter the enemy. He has revealed to us His resources for resisting the enemy's attacks. By the inspiration of the Holy Spirit, He has also identified the major pitfalls of which last-day believers especially should be aware. Paul outlines them in 1 Corinthians, chapter 10. Let's look at it again:

> Moreover, brethren, I do not want you to be unaware that all our fathers were under the cloud, all passed through the sea, all were baptized into Moses in the cloud and in the sea, all ate the same spiritual food, and all drank the same spiritual drink. For they drank of that spiritual Rock that followed them, and that Rock was Christ. But with most of them God was not well pleased, for their bodies were scattered in the wilderness. Now these things became our examples, to the intent that we should not lust after evil things as they also lusted. And do not become

idolaters as were some of them. As it is written, *"The people sat down to eat and drink, and rose up to play."* Nor let us commit sexual immorality, as some of them did, and in one day twenty-three thousand fell; nor let us tempt Christ, as some of them also tempted, and were destroyed by serpents; nor murmur, as some of them also murmured, and were destroyed by the destroyer.

Now all these things happened to them as examples, and they were written for our admonition, on whom the ends of the ages have come. Therefore let him who thinks he stands take heed lest he fall. No temptation has overtaken you except such as is common to man; but God is faithful, who will not allow you to be tempted beyond what you are able, but with the temptation will also make the way of escape, that you may be able to bear it. Therefore, my beloved, flee from idolatry. I speak as to wise men; judge for yourselves what I say (vv. 1–13).

In the pages of *The Great Compromise,* we have closely examined the chief areas of compromise that cost the Israelites their opportunity to enter the Promised Land. Because Paul especially noted that the words he wrote were for those "on whom the ends of the ages have come"—last-day believers—I believe we should take very special heed of these detailed warnings contained in 1 Corinthians, chapter 10.

When the Thrill is Gone

We already know that no one falls away from the Lord overnight. We know, from what we have learned together in *The Great Compromise,* that falling away is a process that usually transpires over the passage of time. To put it in biblical terminology, it's called *backsliding*. It happens when "the thrill is gone"—when the "spiritual romance" begins to ebb. Christianity is no longer exciting and fun, but boring and a drudge. When spiritual things are no longer quite as appealing as they once were, that old lifestyle starts looking good again. Glamorous! Exciting!

Nobody calls their Christian friend and says, "Hey—I feel like backsliding. Want to come along? We could go out drinking and maybe turn into a couple of alcoholics. Does that sound good? Or maybe we could be unfaithful to our wives, destroy our marriages, disappoint our kids, and take a wrecking ball to our homes. Sound good? Pick you up around 10:00 P.M.!" No—that just isn't how it happens. The onset of backsliding is more subtle than that.

Granted, there may be some dimwits who dive right in to Satan's trap, but Satan is no fool. He rarely plays his hand in such an obvious way as to show you what he really has waiting up his sleeve. Instead, he will attempt to deceive you by leading you, one step at a time, through a series of compromises, until he has you right where he wants you—by the throat.

First, you stopped going to church on a regular basis. You began checking in now and then when you felt like it, until you didn't feel like it very often. Then you began reducing the time you spent with other Christians, and increasing your time around unbelievers. At first you reasoned that you were just being a good witness. You told yourself that you were being the "salt" of the earth.

Then one day you realized that this slow, downward spiral had landed you in the midst of a spiritual wilderness—a dry place where God felt distant and you began to wonder if you were ever a believer at all. Whose fault is it that you are now in a spiritual wilderness? God's? The devil's? No—yours!

How Did it Happen that You Fell Away?

You may protest and say, "But wait! I didn't want to fall away—the devil overpowered me!" Though I am not discounting the devil's considerable power and participation in the process, I am saying to you that in your heart of hearts, you know you lowered your guard and made some deliberate and very foolish moves. Come on—admit it. You are responsible—just like the Israelites. The Israelites' failure to reach the Promised Land did not result from God's inadequate provision. Nor was it the result of a lack of direction. It was the direct result of their own compromise. Instead of staying close to the Lord, as they should have, they began to move away—inch by inch—until they began to play by their own spiritual rules.

Scripture teaches, "No temptation has seized you except what is common to man. And God is faithful; he will not let you be tempted beyond what you can bear. But when you are tempted, he will also provide a way out so that you can stand up under it" (1 Cor. 10:13, NIV). When God lets His children go through fiery trials, He will be right there with them in the midst of those trials. He knows what we can handle.

The night Jesus was arrested in the Garden of Gethsemane, He knew the trials ahead were severe, even crushing, and that His disciples could not bear up under them. So He prevented His disciples from being arrested with Him, in order to fulfill what He had said previously: "Of those whom you gave Me I have lost none" (see John 6:39). Jesus knew the disciples were not ready for such a severe test. But in time, they would be ready for even more. According to church history, all the apostles—with the exception of John—died the deaths of martyrs. Yet God knew that in this tender moment—as they watched their Master being taken away—to be arrested along with Him would have overwhelmed them.

Are you in a critical moment right now? Rest assured, God knows your limitations. He will never let you down. He does not sit in heaven and play games like, "Eenie, meenie, miney, moe! This one will make it, and this one won't!" No—He's faithful. Everything you need to grow and flourish and even make your desert bloom again has been given to you in God's Word, which states, "His divine power has given to us all things that pertain to life and godliness . . ." (2 Pet. 1:3).

God has given the potential and provided the resources for each of us to thrive in the Christian life. The question is, what will we do with them?

Without question, each of us has the capacity to fall—and fall hard. We have already established that truth. We would do well, then, to be especially aware of Paul's warning to the church in Romans, chapter 13: "The night is nearly over, the day has almost dawned. Let us therefore fling away the things that men do in the dark, let us arm ourselves for the fight of the day! . . . Let us be Christ's men from head to foot, and give no chances to the flesh to have its fling" (Rom. 13:12, 14, PHILLIPS).

LET'S PRAY

If your Christian walk has become more like a playground than a battlefield, will you make a recommitment to Jesus Christ? This spiritual war is one that will rage, whether or not you take part in it. Don't be listed as a statistic, under the column marked "casualties."

Father, I ask You to forgive me for wandering off the beaten path and into a spiritual wilderness. I have let down my guard. I have let compromise weaken my walk with You. Please restore me. Help me to faithfully attend church, study Your Word, and fight the good fight of faith. I want to be listed as a warrior for the Lord, not as a casualty of the devil! Thank You for making me "strong in the Lord, and in the power of His might." In Jesus' name, I pray. Amen.

10

RUN WITH ENDURANCE
AND FIGHT TO WIN

Let us run with endurance the race that is set before us, looking unto Jesus . . . who for the joy that was set before Him endured the cross, despising the shame, and has sat down at the right hand of the throne of God.

—Hebrews 12:1–2

Have you ever run a marathon? If you have ever experienced running in one of these milestone athletic events, you know what is required just to participate. You start training months ahead of time. You jog. You lift weights. You build up your endurance to increase your distance running. You watch your diet. Just before running, you decrease your fat intake and increase your "carbos." Experienced runners call this strange dietary gear-shift taking on a "carbo load." Now you're ready— almost. Time for a trip to the local mall to upgrade your running gear. The latest in athletic apparel. New running shoes. *Now* you're ready!

But new running clothes won't cut it if you haven't trained for the marathon. No training . . . no victory. Without training, you probably won't last the first mile. Sorry to burst your bubble, but that's just how it is.

That's also how it is in our race to the spiritual finish line. Hebrews, chapter 12, states, "Therefore we also, since we are surrounded by so great a cloud of witnesses, let us lay aside every weight, and the sin which so easily ensnares us, and let us run with endurance the race that is set before us, looking unto Jesus, the author and finisher of our faith, who for the joy that was set before Him endured the cross, despising the shame, and has sat down at the right hand of the throne of God. For consider Him who endured such hostility from sinners against Himself, lest you become weary and discouraged in your souls" (vv. 1–3).

In this passage of text, Paul presents an interesting picture, often using athletic analogies to compare the faith walk—or race—with a runner's ability to last all the way to the finish line. Paul maintains that the Christian lifestyle is a race, a struggle—a fight from beginning to end.

He makes the same point in 1 Corinthians, chapter 9, when he states, "Do you not know that in a race the runners run but only one gets the prize? Run in such a way as to get the prize. Everyone who competes in the games goes into strict training. They do it to get a crown that will not last; but we do it to get a crown that will last forever. Therefore I do not run like a man running aimlessly; I do not fight like a man beating the air. No, I beat my body and make it my slave so that after I have preached to others, I myself will not be disqualified for the prize" (vv. 24–27, NIV).

Interesting, don't you think? You can see how much Paul wanted to win. He really went after that spiritual prize—not so he could add some new trophy to his wall of fame, or win some shiny new ribbon—but so he could receive an eternal prize. Most importantly, he wanted one day to hear Jesus say, "Well done, thou good and faithful servant, Paul—well done!" To Paul, that was the top prize that made all the training, all the pain of muscle burn, all the hardship of building endurance for the run, worth it. And it's the same for sincere, committed believers in every age. It should be what we all long for.

Apparently, the believers addressed by the Author in the Book of Hebrews were experiencing some discouragement. Perhaps they were slowing down. Cooling off in fervor. Backpedaling. Maybe some were even thinking about giving up the faith. To those believers, the Holy Spirit was saying, "Come on, now. Get up! Keep running! Don't quit!"

Our Spiritual Race

To the Christian, the race of faith represents a whole lot more than a simple long-distance run. To get an accurate picture, we must think of it as a cross-country run riddled with obstacles strewn in its path—obstacles designed to trip us up. To get to the end of a course like that will require real commitment.

It reminds me of my school days, when I went out for track and field. I was very good at short-distance runs, but I really lacked something in the long distance department. I would start out with high hopes at the sound of the starting pistol. In fact, I'd leave everybody else in the dust. I would be running along at a pretty good clip—out there in front of everyone else—when something would happen. Just about the time I was feeling good about the fact that all the other runners were eating *my* dust, I would inevitably become winded and start to ease up. Soon runner after runner passed *me* up.

This was no 50-yard dash. This was distance running—eight or nine laps at least. With each passing lap, I lagged further and further behind . . . until the other runners had lapped me once . . . lapped me twice. By the end of the race, I was barely chugging. I huffed and puffed. My lungs burned with pain. My arms and legs felt loose, like rubber. It was hard for me to finish races like these because I never learned to pace myself. From the word "go," I gave it all I had; but somewhere around the end of the second lap, I ran out of steam.

In the spiritual race, speed is certainly important, but so is finishing. If we're going to finish the race, we must not grow weary but learn to pace ourselves. It is something that will take commitment. In Philippians, chapter 3, Paul wrote, "Brothers, I do not consider myself yet to have taken hold of it. But one thing I do: Forgetting what is behind and straining toward what is ahead, I press on toward the goal to win the prize for which God has called me heavenward in Christ Jesus." He is telling believers that at times this will be hard to do. At times it will hurt. The picture here is of a runner whose muscles are cramped and burning, but who persists in pressing toward the goal—getting across the finish line—no matter what.

To win, we must run fast. We must run hard. We must run long. And we must run all the way to the end. As I mentioned earlier, it's a fight—the fight of faith—a fight to the finish. But God has given us both the motivation and the model.

"Therefore, since we are surrounded by such a great cloud of witnesses . . ." begins Hebrews, chapter 12 (NIV). What a model!

Here are history's heroes and heroines of the faith. Lest we think we're the only ones who ever had to face difficulties in order to finish the race of faith, the Bible reminds us in the Book of Hebrews of those whose faith cost them everything. That "hall of faith" includes such men and women as Enoch, who "walked with God and was no more;" Noah, who preserved life inside the ark when God sent a forty-day deluge; Abraham, "friend of God," and his wife, Sarah, whose faith pleased God and produced a son in their old age.

Moses. Elijah. Daniel. Jeremiah. Stephen. Paul. Some of these were martyred for the faith. They endured stonings, scourgings, and some were crucified. Hear what Scripture says about these great men and women of faith: "What more shall I say? For the time would fail me to tell of Gideon and Barak and Samson and Jephtath, also of David and Samuel and the prophets: who through faith subdued kingdoms, worked righteousness, obtained promises, stopped the mouths of lions, quenched the violence of fire, escaped the edge of the sword, out of weakness were made strong, became valiant in battle, and turned to flight the armies of the aliens. Women received their dead raised to life again. And others were tortured, not accepting deliverance, that they might obtain a better resurrection. Still others had trial of mockings and scourgings, yes, and of chains and imprisonment. They were stoned, they were sawn in two, were tempted, were slain with the sword. They wandered about in sheepskins and goatskins, being destitute, afflicted, tormented—of whom the world was not worthy. They wandered in deserts and mountains, in dens and caves of the earth" (Heb. 11:32–38).

These are among that "cloud of witnesses," cheering you on to the finish line. Doesn't that make you want to buy new track shoes?

We Need the Right Equipment

If we are to fight the fight of faith and complete the race to the finish, we must have the right equipment. God provided everything we'll need to equip us in Scripture. We have "the whole armor of God" (Eph. 6:11). We have the mind of Christ (see Phil. 2:5). We have the blood of Christ (see Heb. 9:14). We have Jesus as our Intercessor (see Rom. 8:26). We have the Word of God—the sword of the Spirit—in our mouths (see Rom. 10:8).

Now, if this were a real footrace, we would need the right shoes. Not just any shoes, mind you. We'd need running shoes. Personally, I like Nikes. I recently went to one of their new mega-stores to purchase a new pair. This huge store had multi-levels and hi-tech gadgetry galore. Huge video screens . . . futuristic displays . . . all primarily selling shoes. I never knew 'til then that there were so many kinds of Nikes on the market. All I wanted was a pair of plain white Nikes. I asked the salesman, "How many types of Nikes do you sell?" "Three hundred—and then some," he replied. Some with air. Some without. Some in colors. Some black. Some white. I told the salesman I wanted white ones.

"What kind?" he asked. *"White!"* I stated again. "No, what kind of shoes?" "Running shoes," I answered. "How many kinds of those do you have on hand?" I asked. I discovered Nike made so many kinds of white running shoes that I was absolutely overwhelmed. The salesman continued: "There are different types of running shoes. These are for a certain kind of running," he said, motioning to one pair of white Nikes. "If you run on asphalt, you'll need these," he said, motioning to a different group of shoes. "If you run on gravel, then this is the shoe for you," he said, proudly holding up a white Nike. To me, it looked exactly like all the others, but to this salesman, it was one-of-a-kind—unique. "If you plan to play basketball, may I suggest these shoes?" He pointed to an array of white Nikes, each a little different from the next. I couldn't make a decision. So I left. In essence, I gave up on a new pair of Nikes—at least, for the time being.

But I plan to stay in the spiritual race. I want the prize, don't you? To run to win, don't forget—you will need the right equipment.

The Quality of Endurance

Let's look at Hebrews, chapter 12, verse 1: "Let us lay aside every weight, and the sin which so easily ensnares us, and let us run with endurance the race that is set before us." Endurance. What a powerful word in the Greek. In Greek, the word is *hupemone*. It can be translated to mean "steady determination." It defines the person who, with consistency and steady determination, will not be swerved from his or her course by circumstances, trials, setbacks, or hardships. No matter what obstacles come up to be dealt with, this type of person persists. They stick with God, no matter what.

Interestingly enough, it is during times of trial and hardship that the quality of endurance is produced. James 1:2–3 (NIV) states: "Consider it pure joy, my brothers, whenever you face trials of many kinds, because you know that the testing of your faith develops perseverance." There's that Greek word, *hupemone,* again, speaking of "steadfastness." It is the trying and testing of your faith which will produce this quality. And perseverance must finish its work so that you—the believer, set on finishing the race of faith before you—will be properly equipped to complete it. To finish, you will need endurance; and trials are building that quality within you.

No one I know likes to endure trials and testing. I don't like it. Do you? I don't like hardship. Who does? I like it when things go smoothly.

But I must admit that the times when I experienced the most growth were the times when things were tough. Where do we develop these inner qualities that produce depth and character and endurance? In the midst of tests and trials. James writes, "Consider it pure joy . . . whenever you face trials." Now, I don't know about actually rejoicing over trials and testing. But I certainly agree in principle because I know we grow spiritually during these difficult times.

Little by little, we are built up by the trials. It's a lot like running. When we first start to run, our muscles begin to burn before we barely make a lap around the track. It hurts so bad, it throbs. But if we keep at it, pretty soon we'll be able to do two laps, then three, then more before our muscles starting shouting, "Stop! Pain! Help! Quit! No!" Soon we even stop listening altogether to those wimpy messages our muscles are telegraphing. Why? Because we are developing endurance. We are becoming stronger because we have spent time in training. As they say, "No pain . . . no gain." Now we're on the "gain" side of the pain.

Of course, we may choose not to train and instead look for a shortcut. But let me state right now that there are no shortcuts to spiritual victory. Only through difficulties is endurance built.

There is no shortcut to achieving it. So don't recoil at the first sight of problems. Don't run for cover. God has a plan. He wants to strengthen you, toughen you up for spiritual battle, make you a "long-distance runner" in the race of faith.

Cruise-control faith won't cut it in this spiritual race. Bare minimum performance will be eaten up in the dust of other, more committed runners. If you plan to finish, determine right now to do whatever it takes to make it across the finish line. Second Peter, chapter 1 says, "My brothers, be all the more eager to make your calling and election sure. For if you do these things, you will never fall, and you will receive a rich welcome into the eternal kingdom of our Lord and Savior Jesus Christ" (vv. 10–11, NIV). That's the prize! That's what I want! How about you?

God Has a Lane Marked out For You

Remember this—when you run the race of faith, you are not in competition with other believers. Your real competition is *the devil, and your own sinful nature.* You have a lane already marked out for you—a lane prepared just for you by God. He has it all lined up and waiting for you. Only you can run within the confines of that lane. And I have a lane, which I must run within. No lane switching allowed!

Please don't try to impress or outrun me. Don't try to make me eat dust. I'm not in competition with you. Yes, it's true that we have certain things in common. But it is also true that God has prepared different work for each believer to perform in the course of his or her "race." Say you and I are running alongside each other in our own individually marked running lanes, and you see me fall. Do you point at me and laugh as you kick some more dust on me? Or do you stop, turn around, extend a hand, and offer to help me up? Remember—we are in competition with the devil—not each other. If you fall down, I want to help you get up. If all believers would focus on helping each other, as if they were members of the same team, instead of engaging in name-calling, finger-pointing, and other forms of betrayal, the devil would take a major hit—instead of the other way around. He wants us to fight each other instead of the "good fight of faith."

Learn to Travel Light

In 2 Timothy 4:7–8, Paul wrote, "I have fought the good fight, I have finished the race, I have kept the faith. Finally, there is the crown of righteousness, which the Lord, the righteous Judge, will give to me on that Day, laid up for me and not to me only but also to all who have loved His appearing." But many believers aren't finishing—they're falling. They're not winning—they're crashing and burning. Why is that? Some fall because they are encumbered with too much "weight." Just as it is possible for a person to be physically overweight and thereby damage their health and shorten their life expectancy, so it is possible to be spiritually overweight. If we plan to finish this spiritual race we are in, we must learn to travel light.

As a nation, it's no secret that America is consumed with weight. It seems that everyone (myself included) would like to be a bit thinner. We go on diets, deprive ourselves of real food, opting instead for low-fat versions that sacrifice much in the way of taste and texture but help us keep the bulges at bay. Weight-loss clinics, weight-loss formulas, weight-loss gimmicks, weight-loss pills, equipment, systems, gadgets, shakes—you name it, we've tried it. Then we lose interest, and that spare tire gently falls back around our waists . . . again. How many pieces of home exercise equipment have *you* bought, then lost interest in and stuck out in the garage, where they remain, collecting dust?

Just as it's difficult to lug around all those extra pounds if you are overweight physically, it is also difficult to lug around those extra spiritual pounds.

My ministry as an evangelist has required that I travel a great deal for many years. I still haven't got the luggage thing down right. I always take too much stuff with me. Then I have to carry it around. It can get wearisome. First, I take a lot of books. Books are heavy. They're like bricks. Do you know how heavy a suitcase filled with books can get after you've been lugging it around for a couple of hours? But I just have to have those books with me, so I bite the bullet and pack them, even though I know I'm the one who'll be required to tote them around. Then I add to that load my computer and add-ons.

After I've been lugging them around for awhile, I say to myself, *"Greg, why did you bring that piece of junk? You don't need it."* The answer is simple: that's just the way I am. Ever been there?

But I also know this about myself: I have stuff, not the other way around. If I were flying at an altitude of 15,000 feet aboard a jet and the captain began to announce, "We have just lost power in three of our four engines and we need to get rid of some extra weight," you can believe I'd ditch everything I had on board out the nearest shoot. If jettisoning a few pounds of baggage would mean the difference between landing safely and watching the ground rise up to meet me, I'd choose dumping the baggage.

Well, something as significant as that is happening in this spiritual race. It is a fight to the finish. It is a matter of spiritual life or death. If you're carrying a bunch of old baggage—stuff like bitterness, unforgiveness, anger, hurt, and more—stuff that will only weigh you down and slow you down. Why not stop and dump it before you crash and burn?

What are some of the weights that can slow us down spiritually? Sometimes it's things that, in and of themselves, are not bad. But watch it if you begin to overindulge. Something that wasn't created to be evil can become an evil influence. It can start slowing you down. It's a weight. It has become sinful. Cast it aside and keep going. Cast off that pursuit that is going nowhere, that pastime, that relationship that's slowing you down and holding you back from the finish line.

A weight is anything that would tear the people of God away from Him or dull their spiritual hunger for His Word. It's anything that would dull their desire for prayer or take away their spiritual appetites for the things of God. Anything that reduces the importance of Bible study and makes this world system more attractive is a weight.

Perhaps it will help you if I share my own method of determining whether something is harmless or harmful. I have prepared a checklist that I use from time to time to help me make the right decisions in some of life's grey areas. Consider applying these four principles to help you choose the best course to follow:

1. *Does it build me up spiritually?* What do you do with your free time? You have a choice, you know. You can use it in ways

that will increase and enhance your spiritual walk with the Lord or you can use it up on things that have no lasting value. What programming do you listen to on your car radio while you drive? Just music—or Christian music? Even better, why not a good Christian station featuring solid teaching? You have control over what you are exposed to. Just remember the old computer-age adage: *Garbage in . . . garbage out!* Your mind is like one giant computer that is receiving input at all times. What are you inputting into your computer? What are you feeding into your heart . . . your mind? Are you inputting things that will benefit you eternally, or empty "junk" information that will only slow you down?

2. Does it bring me under its power? Remember, Paul wrote, "All things are lawful unto me, but all things are not expedient" (1 Cor. 6:12, KJV). I don't know about you, but I choose not to be under the power of anything or anyone except Jesus Christ, my Lord. I don't want to be under the power of food. I don't want to be under the power of television. I don't want to be under the power of gambling. I don't want to be under the power of alcohol. I don't need those things.

Yet I constantly hear Christians trying to find loopholes to cover things like social drinking. "It's OK if I just have a glass of wine now and then . . . isn't it? Or a 'brewski' with the boys?" My answer to questions like those is, "Why?" Why drink if you don't plan to be under the power of alcohol? If you drink at all—even one glass of wine—you're a whole lot closer to being under the power of alcohol than if you just avoid it altogether. After all, it's hard to get drunk if you don't drink! Why see how close to the edge you can get without falling off? For that matter, why settle for a cheap substitute when God promises, "Don't be drunk with wine, but be filled with the Holy Spirit" (see Eph. 5:18). There is nothing greater than that.

3. Do I have an uneasy conscience about it? Now, this is a tricky one. Romans 14:23 (KJV) says, "Whatsoever is not of faith is sin." Another way to translate this verse is, "Whatever is done without conviction of its approval by God is sinful." There may be some area where there are no clear-cut biblical guidelines. It seems all right, and other Christians you know are doing it, so you proceed. If, however, your conscience remains troubled and uneasy—that's your cue to shut everything down. Stop right there before your mind starts rationalizing: *Wait a minute— so-and-so is doing it!* Yes, but so-and-so is not you. If you proceed when your conscience says "stop," you may follow so-and-so straight into the path of compromise.

4. *Could it cause someone else to stumble?* This is perhaps the most important question of all. We are in this race to bring other souls to Christ, not to keep them away. We must not create any stumbling blocks for our brothers and sisters in Christ. Not everyone is tripped up by the same sins, you know. For one person, it may be lust. For another, the stumbling block may be greed. Another person may look at someone who has a problem with lust or greed and say, "Thank God, I would never do those things!" What's *his* problem? Pride! So there are plenty of stumbling blocks out there to go around. The challenge is to live in such a way that you do not place stumbling blocks in the way of your fellow believers.

What Now?

Yes, we all have our areas of vulnerability. We all have weights, or things that slow us down. We are confronted daily by a wide array of compromises that potentially could shut us down completely. How do we deal with that? We lay aside those weights.

Paul said, "Lay aside the weight and sin that so easily besets you." Lay it aside! You don't have to continue doing that thing that is hanging up your Christian walk. You don't have to continually expose yourself to temptation. You don't have to keep on compromising. It's not as if there is some set-in-stone pattern that is impossible for you to break out of. The Bible is filled with promises for just such occasions. Take, for example, this insightful word from Scripture: "Our soul has escaped as a bird from the snare of the fowlers: the snare is broken, and we have escaped. Our help is in the name of the Lord, who made heaven and earth" (Ps. 124:7–8). Can you see it? God provides a way of escape in every situation—even yours.

"But Greg," you say, "That's easy for you to say. You're a preacher. You pastor your little church and read your little books and live cloistered in your Christian sub-culture all day. I live in the real world. I'm out there in the work force. I have to deal with nonbelievers all day long and hear them curse and watch the way they live."

We both know you can't control your environment at all times, or the kinds of people you will encounter. But you can make up for it in how you choose to spend your free time, because you can control that.

How do you finish the race and make it safely across the finish line? By "looking to Jesus, the author and finisher of our faith, who for the joy that was set before Him endured the cross, despising the shame. . ." (Heb. 12:2). Look to Jesus—that's how you do it. Fix your eyes on Him. Refuse to look at anything else but Him. Deliberately tune out all the distractions. Focus!

Keep Your Eyes on Jesus

Simon Peter walked on water the night that frightening storm blew through the Sea of Galilee. He didn't sink as long as he kept his eyes on Jesus. But the minute he looked away to the turbulent waves, the lightning, and the rolling sea, he began to sink. Perhaps it was the sound of thunder that caused Peter to take his eyes off the Lord. We'll never know. Maybe it was when he looked down at the tossing of the waves. Whatever it was that broke his concentration, Peter was gripped by sudden panic. And that's when he began to sink. He cried out, "Lord, save me!" And of course, Jesus did.

Paul and Silas knew the secret of focusing on Jesus. Instead of moaning and groaning about the pain and deprivation they were experiencing as prisoners in a Roman jail, they fixed their eyes on Jesus—and began to sing His praises! I'd say that's rising above your circumstances, wouldn't you? That's definitely faith over fear. That's saying, "I can't change my circumstances, but God is still on the throne. I'm still His child. I'm still going to heaven. He will see me through, so I'm just going to praise Him!" The Bible records that in the midst of their late-night prayer and praise meeting, the earth shook, the prison doors opened, and an angel of the Lord appeared to lead them to safety. Salvation broke out too. The jailor was so moved by what he had seen and heard that he immediately inquired, "Sirs, what must I do to be saved?" (Acts 16:30).

When you look at Jesus, your problems fall into the right perspective. They no longer loom over you so overwhelmingly. Get your eyes off them and fix them on Jesus. He will never leave you nor forsake you. He will see you safely across the finish line of this race that is actually a spiritual battle.

Others may attempt to discourage you. They may taunt, "You'll never make it! You're going to fail! You'll just crash and burn!" But if you refuse to listen to them and keep looking at Jesus, the "author and finisher of your faith," you'll make it.

I like the words of Corrie ten Boom, who knew a bit about suffering. A Dutch Christian, she was imprisoned in a Nazi death camp because she and her family had aided the escape of Jews from the Nazis. Rightly so, the ten Booms believed the Jews were God's chosen people. They opened their home to hide Jewish families until they could make their way out of war-torn Europe. When the Nazis discovered "the hiding place," the ten Booms were arrested. All but Corrie were killed. Safe on the other side of all that incredible suffering, she summed it up with these brief words:

"Look within and be depressed;
Look without and be distressed;
Look at Jesus and be at rest."[1]

There's Still Time to Turn it Around

Consider the example of Alfred Nobel, inventor of the explosive, dynamite. One morning while Nobel was reading the morning paper, he was shocked to discover his own obituary. Someone at the newspaper had obviously made a great error and falsely reported that he had died. You might say that Alfred Nobel was given a luxury that few people will ever receive: a chance to see what's said about him after his death. What he read was not pleasing to Alfred Nobel.

The obituary primarily remembered him as the man who had invented dynamite, which had been used as a weapon of warfare, killing many thousands. It turned his blood to ice to think that above all his other accomplishments in life, he would be remembered as the man who gave the world its most destructive weapon. Then and there, he determined that he would make some changes in his life. Nobel made a personal vow: "From this day forward, I will dedicate my life to the pursuit of peace."

Creator of the Nobel Peace Prize, today when we hear of Alfred Nobel, we no longer think of dynamite, but of peace.

As you examine your spiritual life, how would you describe it? Would you describe yourself as strong? Weak? About to give up? Before you become discouraged and fall out of the race entirely, give it one more shot. Put everything you have into it. Give it your all, or one day you may wake up and realize that you wasted and squandered the resources and potential God placed within you.

Let's Finish the Race

Let's stop making lame excuses and finish the race, shall we? Let's stop blaming others, circumstances, even the devil. Let's just look to Jesus, "who for the joy that was set before him endured the cross, despising the shame, and is set down at the right hand of the throne of God" (Heb. 12:2, KJV).

When Jesus carried that weighty, cumbersome cross through the winding streets of Jerusalem and to Golgotha, where He was nailed to it and left to die a horrible, painful death, it was a shameful thing. People laughed at Him. They mocked Him. They cursed Him. They wanted nothing to do with Him as He hung there, dying. Most of His disciples had forsaken Him. All but John were nowhere to be found that day. What kept Him going? What made Him bear up under all that horrible abuse? The Bible says it was "the joy that was set before Him." What joy? The joy of knowing that His death would set men free of Satan's clutches, traps, and snares.

Remember—there is joy in heaven each time a sinner comes to Christ (see Luke 15:7). So why did Jesus press through to the finish line that day at Calvary?

For you.

LET'S PRAY

Are there so-called weights that have beset you as you press toward the finish line of this spiritual race? Are there things that are slowing you down? Let's pray:

Father, I ask You to help me lay aside the weights in my life—things I may not even realize are dangerous. Show me what must go as I prayerfully seek You. Help me to let go of those compromising things that are causing me to hang back—things that may potentially cause my brothers and sisters in Christ to stumble. I pray for endurance, Lord. Help me to finish the race. Help me to fight to win! In Jesus' name, I pray. Amen.

11

FIGHT TO THE FINISH

Fight the good fight of faith, lay hold on eternal life, to which you were also called and have confessed the good confession in the presence of many witnesses.

—1 Timothy 6:12

Have you ever been tempted to quit while you're ahead? Sure. We all have. There are times when it seems we're not going to make it to the finish. So we think about all the angles, count the cost, and sometimes determine to cut our losses, regroup, and settle for less than what we would have received, had we hung in 'til the end. For some individuals, this is a mentality.

A good example is the person who drops out of college a couple of credits shy of graduation. It seemed like a good idea at the time. After all, that good-paying job offer came along, and taking it meant you could get married now instead of later, settle down, and start a family. But that great-paying job you might have had if you had finished your degree just never materialized. It would have been a struggle to stay in college. But now—twenty years later—you're sorry you didn't. That's what I mean by this "quit while you're ahead" mentality.

Let me illustrate this concept with a story from the Bible—the story of Moses and his confrontations with the Egyptian Pharaoh over the issue of Israel's deliverance from bondage. Pharaoh tried to convince the Israelites to quit while they were ahead—to settle for less. But Moses said, "Nothing doing!" God had spoken to Moses and made it very clear that he was to march into Pharaoh's court and demand the complete, unconditional release of all the Israelites. He instructed them to make a three-day journey into the wilderness to have a feast before the Lord and make sacrifices. Pharaoh's heart had hardened. At first, Pharaoh would hear nothing of granting Moses' request. Then, after the manifestation of a series of miracles, he tried to cut a deal.

Here is a picture of the devil, who is always unwilling to let his captives go. He'd like to cut a deal, if we would settle for one.

A stubborn man, Pharaoh's heart grew harder and harder each time Moses appeared before him as a spokesman for God. With each rejection of the will of God, his heart grew as cold as stone. When Moses delivered God's command to "Let My people go," he said pridefully, "Who is the Lord that I should obey His voice to let Israel go? I do not know the Lord, nor will I let Israel go" (Ex. 5:2).

As if to underscore his authority over the people he had made his slaves, Pharaoh issued a harsh new edict, stepping up the production of the bricks the Jews were required to make to keep his lavish construction projects going. Only this time, the slaves were to be required to make their bricks without the benefit of straw—the necessary binding ingredient to hold the materials together. Now not only had Pharaoh refused to let the people go, but he was requiring them to work harder than ever.

God gave Pharaoh every chance to yield to His clearly stated demands, as delivered by Moses. Each time, Pharaoh turned a deaf ear. The Bible tells us that God "is longsuffering toward us, not willing that any should perish but that all should come to repentance" (2 Pet. 3:9). But when the grace ran out for Pharaoh, God began to deal with him via harsher terms.

A series of plagues then befell Egypt. Frogs, lice, darkness, boils, and burning hail vexed the entire population, simply because one hard-hearted man refused to obey God. Each time he saw a miracle performed through Moses or Aaron, Pharaoh had a fresh chance to heed God's demands. Each time, however, his heart grew harder and colder. Pharaoh continued to resist . . . and resist. The plagues increased in intensity, until the final one—death to the firstborn sons of all the houses in the land of Egypt. No one's firstborn son was exempt—not even Pharaoh's. The tragic death of his son and successor would never have been necessary if Pharaoh had simply bowed his knee before the Most High God.

Finally he began to wheel and deal with Moses: "All right, all right! Go and sacrifice to the Lord, but stay here in Egypt. Egypt is a great place! There's no need to leave."

But Moses said, "Nothing doing!

Again Pharaoh tried to lower the stakes. "Okay, you can go— but don't go far."

And again, Moses said, "No way! We're going all the way into the wilderness, where we will make our sacrifices."

Obviously, Pharaoh still did not want to let the Jews leave Egypt. After all, he would be losing his best slaves. He offered Moses another "bargain." "I'll let you go, but the kids and the cattle stay here! Once more Moses held out for complete obedience to God's commands to the Israelites. "We're taking the children and the cattle, and all of our possessions, for that matter!"

Can't You Just Hear the Devil?

The devil does the same thing to believers. He certainly didn't want to lose you in the first place—that's for sure. But if he can't drag you into hell with him, he would at least like to immobilize you. The devil well knows that a committed, on-fire believer is a sure threat to his kingdom. Thus the devil, like Pharaoh, will try to strike a compromise. "All right, all right! You've given your life to Jesus Christ. Fine. I didn't want you to do that, but I can live with it."

He may whisper in your ear, "Just stay cool. You don't need to go to church every Sunday, do you? Besides, the surf's up. Why not go surfing? Or play golf? Can't God hear you out on the water or on the links as easily as in a pew? Can't you worship God better if you're out there in nature? After all, He's all around you. You don't need to be inside a building in order to worship God! Just believe and that's enough. It's OK to still live the way you want to live."

See how subtle that is? Like Pharaoh, Satan also does not wish to let his slaves go free. He wants to keep believers under his thumb, long after they have given their hearts to Christ.

One way he does it is through compromise. He sets us up to go against what we know is right and true. He doesn't want us to break with our old friends. He doesn't want us to make any dramatic changes in our lifestyles. The devil would always like us to give just a little . . . here . . . and there . . . and everywhere . . . until we're caught beneath a "compromise pileup." He spends a lot of time selling us lies like this: "All right, let's be practical. Believe in God if you must, but let's not go overboard! Don't become a religious fanatic!"

Many believers have fallen into this trap. They ask Christ into their lives, yet continue to hang out with their old friends and conduct business as usual in every other area of their lives. They do the same things they always did. Their life really never goes through the transformation that must transpire if one truly aspires to know God.

The devil will whisper, "Okay—believe if you want. Just don't go too far away."

That's what Pharaoh said to Moses. Let's look at Scripture to see how clever was Pharaoh's wheeling and dealing with Israel's great deliverer:

> Then Pharaoh called for Moses and Aaron, and said, "Go, sacrifice to your God in the land." And Moses said, "It is not right to do so, for we would be sacrificing the abomination of the Egyptians to the Lord our God. If we sacrifice the abomination of the Egyptians before their eyes, then will they not stone us? We will go three days' journey into the wilderness and sacrifice to the Lord our God as He will command us." And Pharaoh said, "I will let you go, that you may sacrifice to the Lord your God in the wilderness; only you shall not go very far away. Intercede for me." Then Moses said, "Indeed I am going out from you, and I will entreat the Lord, that the swarms of flies may depart tomorrow from Pharaoh, from his servants, and from his people. But let Pharaoh not deal deceitfully anymore in not letting the people go to sacrifice to the Lord." So Moses went out from Pharaoh and entreated the Lord. And the Lord did according to the word of Moses; He removed the swarms of flies from Pharaoh, from his servants, and from his people. Not one remained. But Pharaoh hardened his heart at this time also; neither would he let the people go.
> —Exodus 8:25–32

Pharaoh was trying to trick Moses. He was trying to get him to settle for less. He was playing "Let's Make a Deal." "Okay,

Moses—you can go. Take the Israelites, but leave the kids. Leave the cattle. Leave the old folks." But Moses said, "No! We're not going to leave anything behind. And we're not going to make any short-term, part-way deals. It's all or nothing!"

That's the spirit! All or nothing! That's how we believers should be! No deals. No compromises. No settling for less than God's very best for our lives.

Hear what Pharaoh finally tried to offer the Israelites: "Then Pharaoh called to Moses and said, 'Go, serve the Lord; only let your flocks and your herds be kept back. Let your little ones also go with you.' But Moses said, 'You must also give us sacrifices and burnt offerings, that we may sacrifice to the Lord our God. Our livestock shall also go with us; *not a hoof shall be left behind.* For we must take some of them to serve the Lord our God, and even we do not know with what we must serve the Lord until we arrive there'" (Ex. 10:24–26).

What I absolutely love about this passage is that Moses would not back down. Not in the face of intimidation. Not in the face of threats. Not in the face of the fearsome Egyptian Pharaoh. *Not a hoof will be left behind!* I love that! "Pharaoh, you get zero. Nada. Nothing! In fact, now that you mention it, we're going to need a little something to offer as a sacrifice. We'll leave the exact amount up to you. . . . "

The Bible records that when Pharaoh finally let God's people go, they were loaded down with children, old folks, possessions, cattle—and gifts of gold and silver given to them by the Egyptians! How's that for refusing to settle or compromise? Moses, under the Lord's instructions, just kept upping the ante. Instead of backing down, he demanded everything he had previously requested from Pharaoh—and more!

Remember This Example

Take note of this example because the devil uses exactly the same tactics today. He tries to bargain with believers and rip them off, through reasoning. "All right; be a Christian—but stay with me." You say, "No." Then the devil says, "Okay, just give me your children." You say, "No." Then he says, "Then let me have something else that belongs to you."

"No."

"Then let me have some other part of your life."

"No. You don't get anything, devil. Not one thing. You ripped me off before I became a Christian, but you're not going to keep on doing it. Before I met Jesus, you offered me a future filled with nothing but sorrow, suffering, and death. You lied to me. You took advantage of me for years, but now I'm drawing the line. I'm saying 'not a hoof shall be left behind.' I'm not giving up anything. In fact, I'm taking back everything you stole from me in the first place!"

Have you been giving the devil a piece of your life here . . . and another piece there? Have you lowered your guard? Eased a standard? Played with sin? Compromised? Draw the line! Make a break. Take a stand.

If you don't, you're going to be one miserable person. You'll wind up just like Lot—worn down by uncontrolled sin. It's a rip-off. A dead-end street. Don't let it happen to you.

If you have been compromising, playing with sin, letting the devil have your life a piece at a time, there is something you can do. You can rededicate your life to Jesus Christ. You can start anew.

Jesus in Your House

It's a lot like deciding what you'd do if Jesus came to your house. You know He's coming to your door. Now you must decide whether or not you'll answer it. Your heart pounds for a minute as you vacillate back and forth between "yes" and "no." You want Him to come into your heart, because you've talked to others who invited Him in and they spoke of incredible changes that took place in their lives. Yet you're afraid. What if Jesus wants to make changes in your home that you don't want to make?

Suddenly you hear the knock.

He says, "Behold, I stand at the door and knock: if any man hear my voice, and open the door, I will come in to him, and will sup with him, and he with me" (Rev. 3:19, KJV).

You're actually surprised at how quickly you open the door!

Here He is—Jesus—at your door, ready to come in.

You find that you're nervous as He crosses the threshold. You're afraid of what His reaction will be as you slowly show

Him through your dirty, messy home. You notice with new eyes the way your house really looks and try to imagine what must be going through His mind as His clear eyes take it all in. Again, you are surprised that the look on His face does not criticize or condemn. In fact, His expressions seems almost . . . *hopeful!*

After you complete your little tour, you quickly try to route Him back through the living room, which is by far the safest and cleanest of all your rooms. "You left one room out!" He says, knowingly.

Again, you find that your heart is beating wildly as you wonder, *How did He know that?* "I would like to see it now," He persists.

"The door to that one is locked and I've lost the key," you nervously reply.

"Why do you call me Lord and not do what I say?"

Your blood seems to freeze as you realize that He is demanding to peek inside your closet. "But there are *skeletons* in there!" you groan. "I know," He says simply. You mumble something again about the lost key. Then He says, "You have the Master Key in your pocket. If you want Me to take up residence in your home, you must first give me the key that opens every door."

"What about the skeletons?"

"Let's clean them out!"

He seems so confident, so sure of what He is doing, that you reach into your pocket and firmly press that Master Key into the palm of His hand. "Do whatever You must do, Lord."

He moves swiftly. He pulls down all the rotting wallpaper. He picks up every piece of dilapidated furniture you had piled in there and tosses them out the front door. He pulls up all the musty shag carpeting you bought way back in the 60s and tosses it out too. He even throws out your broken lava lamp!

At that point, you interrupt Him. "Excuse me, Lord—this doesn't exactly seem fair. I know this stuff may not look like much to you. It may be old and rotten, but to me, it's all I have. What will I sit on? Where will I sleep?"

Jesus simply puts His hand on your shoulder and smiles down at you before continuing: "Would you mind stepping aside so I could have some more room?"

You step back obediently and watch Jesus as He moves to the front door and lets out a shrill whistle: "Back her up, boys!" He calls, as a huge moving van with the words "Father and Son Moving Company" emblazoned on the side rolls to your door. Then two muscular men begin to carry things in.

First, they lay a huge roll of beautiful new carpet. Next they carry in piece after piece of beautiful, expensive, hand-made furniture—everything so new, it gleams. *Why, everything seems custom made!* you marvel.

After all He's done, you step back to survey the incredible difference Jesus has made. Your closet has been totally cleaned out—but you realize something else. You don't even *have* a closet any longer. Jesus began by cleaning out your closet. Then He totally removed it, as He began to renovate your house. What a dramatic difference His presence has made. Then a new thought dawns on you: *He only took the old things away to give me something better in their place! But first I had to give Him the Master Key.*

Give Him the Key

You can give Him everything—your life, your family, your home, your spouse, your children, your career, your possessions. Retire from managing your own life. Jesus is better at it than you are. Why not let Him take control? Give Him your heart—all of it. Give Him your ambition—He already knows all about it. Give Him your future, because He has it all set up for you. Jeremiah 29:11 says, "For I know the thoughts that I think toward you, says the Lord, thoughts of peace and not of evil, to give you a future and a hope." What a powerful promise!

Give Jesus everything. Leave nothing behind. The Bible states, "Do you not know that . . . you are not your own? For you were bought at a price; therefore glorify God in your body. . ." (1 Cor. 6:19–20). You belong to the Lord! You are His purchased possession. So offer Him the keys to everything you are, everything you have, everything you hope for. Isn't it better to entrust yourself and your most prized possessions into His hands than to play "Let's Make a Deal" with the devil?

Just say, "Here it is, Lord." Then watch what God will do. His plan for your life will surpass your wildest dreams. I can assure you that it will be better than anything you could have planned for yourself. Dedicate yourself. Rededicate your life.

To put this off can place you in the same situation as Pharaoh. Don't let your heart become hard, like his. He had many chances to come to God. He blew every one. Don't let the same thing happen to you. Don't prolong your decision to give Christ free reign in your life. If you hesitate, you may become so calloused by sin and the cares of this world that even the Spirit of God can't penetrate the hardness around your heart. Consider Esau. Here's a man who went beyond the point of no return. Scripture says, "He found no place for repentance, though he sought it diligently with tears" (Heb. 12:17). He allowed his heart to grow irreparably hard. It could happen to you. Don't let it!

A Trip Behind God's Woodshed

Believe me, He is capable of turning us around, even when we're trying our best not to listen. Remember, He loves us and is only looking out for our good. He can see what's ahead down the road, when we humans are blind to those things. He knows what's coming right up, and because He is a loving God, at times there is a need for correction. And He has the ways and the means to see that from time to time we get it.

The Bible says,"Whom the Lord loves He chastens" (Heb. 12:6). Now, no one I know likes to be chastened. I don't like it. Do you? But God's chastening is for our good because He loves us.

The psalmist wrote, "Thy rod and thy staff, they comfort me because the Lord is my Shepherd." Let's use the example of real-life shepherds and their flocks to illustrate this point. In ancient Israel, shepherds used both these instruments—the rod and the staff—to keep their flocks together. A staff is a crooked instrument fashioned with a hook at one end which shepherds used to pull in wayward sheep. Sheep—notoriously stupid—have a habit of occasionally going astray. They just don't know what's good for them. One determined and extremely dense sheep headed for the edge of a cliff will take the whole group along for the ride. Consequently, the shepherd is always having to deal with wayward sheep and use his staff to pull them back into the fold. A rod is nothing more than a club. Shepherds use the rod on *really* wayward sheep—sheep that just won't respond in any other way.

Do you know how sheep are slaughtered? The shepherd uses what is called a "Judas goat" to lead the sheep up the walkway and into the slaughterhouse where they will be killed. The sheep go meekly along, following the Judas goat, not questioning anything. They just comply. That's why the Bible says, "All we like sheep have gone astray; we have turned, every one, to his own way" (Isa. 53:6). Generation after generation, we seem to fall for the same lies, traps, and rip-offs. We get in line behind a new "Judas goat" and follow meekly along the path to destruction. In every generation, we—like sheep—want to look the same, dress the same, talk the same, and believe the same. We wind up headed for the same place—hell . . . or heaven, if we change our direction and follow Jesus Christ.

The psalmist said, "Thy rod and thy staff, they comfort me" (Ps. 23:4, KJV). When we move out of the way, the Good Shepherd will first use a staff—a gentle means—to draw us back into the fold. But let's say we keep resisting that form of correction. Next He'll use the rod.

If you are repeatedly getting into trouble, deliberately crossing the line, then it's time for the rod, friend. If the Good Shepherd has to use it, He will. If you keep wandering away, He'll go after you and use His rod—reluctantly—to render you temporarily helpless and in need of His assistance. Just when you think you've got it covered, *Kapow!* There's the sound of the rod being applied. You may say, "Oh, but that's so cruel!" Shepherds sometimes use the rod to break the legs of a wayward sheep so they will cease their wandering. Better to have a broken leg than to wander off and be consumed by a hungry mountain lion. After he has applied the rod, the shepherd then dresses the wounds, binds them up, and lifts the bleating sheep up onto his shoulders, where he will carry it for the time it takes to heal.

That's how much our Good Shepherd loves us—enough to correct us to keep us from destruction. First, He'll tell us, "That's wrong. Stop doing it. Come on. Quit it. Don't compromise. Stop." If we keep refusing to listen, He'll begin to take stronger measures. Finally, crisis hits. *Kapow!* He nails us with the rod. It's for our own good. Then He'll dress and bind our wounds, lift us onto His shoulders, and carry us until we're well and whole.

Perhaps your life has been hit with crisis recently. Perhaps you have been reaping what you previously sowed. Your sin finally caught up with you. Don't let it destroy you. Rejoice! Let His rod and staff *comfort* you as you are reminded that He loves you enough to warn and correct you! Let it lead you to Jesus. He will help you overcome your crisis and even help you overcome sin. Use this time as a moment of decision. Don't put it off. Do it now.

Don't settle for letting Him have a part of your life and letting the devil have his part too. The Bible says, "Harden not your heart if you can hear his voice." Listen to Him as He calls you to repentance and into a closer walk with Him.

Don't listen to the devil, who will come and try to talk you into waiting until "tomorrow" to make things right with the Lord. Respond now. Today is the "day of salvation" (2 Cor. 6:2, KJV). Today is the day to get real with God on the issue of compromise. Is there compromise in your life? If the answer is "yes," it's time to confront the areas of compromise in your life, repent, and give yourself totally to Jesus. That is the most significant thing you can do to ensure that you will be able to endure the trials that come along. Give yourself totally to Jesus: that is the best thing you can do to help you run with endurance, fight to win, and finish the spiritual race that is set before you.

LET'S PRAY

If you have been settling for giving the devil a piece of your life, why not pray to correct that mistake? Let's pray and rededicate our lives to Jesus:

Father, I come to You a sinner, and I repent of my sin. I rededicate my life to You today. I give You everything I have, everything I am, and I retire from trying to manage my own life. I ask You to manage and direct my life from now on. Help me fight to win. Plan my future. Organize my days. Guide me in Your paths of righteousness, for Your name's sake. Help me to trust that Your plans for me are good, not evil—and better than what I would be willing to settle for if I were choosing my own future. Choose it for me, Lord, and I'll give You the glory. Thank You, Lord. In Jesus' name, I pray. Amen.

12

FINISH WELL

Well done, good and faithful servant . . .
Enter into the joy of your Lord.

—Matthew 25:21

When the great evangelist, C. H. Spurgeon, died in 1892, condolences poured in from all parts of the globe. Here was a man who had won many thousands of souls to Christ. Telegraph wires were jammed with messages to his loved ones, expressing sympathy and tribute to this towering man of God, acclaimed as both the greatest and most popular preacher of the age. To date Spurgeon's sermons stand tall as classics of the faith. His direct style of preaching still cuts through the major issues that have kept men and women from Christ for centuries. His acute spiritual insights break through the barriers and still speak clearly to our hearts and minds.

Known also as a man of meekness, tenderness, and great kindness, Spurgeon was well-loved by the people of his day. Among the first expressions of sympathy to arrive after his death were messages from members of England's royal family—the Prince and Princess of Wales. People from all walks of life sent messages to the loved ones left behind by this man who chose to be buried in an olive casket marked with the words of the great apostle Paul contained in 2 Timothy 4:7:

I have fought the good fight, I have finished my course, I have kept the faith.[1]

When it's time for me to meet Jesus, I wonder—will I be able to say that? Will you?

Not Necessarily a "Photo Finish!"

I want to do a bit better in this spiritual race than I did several years ago in a Father/Son event at my son Christopher's school. I had really been looking forward to this event. After all, I *had* been a track star in the 50-yard dash back in high school! Remember? I relished the opportunity to shine in my son's eyes as I crossed the line in a "photo finish." I could see the sweat pouring off me as I held my arms high, hands clasped in victory. I was smiling. It was great! I could even hear the crowd go wild in cheers and applause. "Hey, that preacher can run pretty fast!"

I bought new running shorts and a new pair of Nike Airs. I was ready! I stood around nonchalantly, waiting for the race to begin. Finally the announcement came over the loud speaker: "All you dads out there, start heading for the starting line!"

My heart was pounding frantically. I wanted to win so badly, but I didn't dare let it show. I sauntered over to the starting line, trying to act cool; then, when the race actually started, I would run like the wind . . . just like the good old days. There at the starting line, I glanced around me and saw how out of shape most of the guys appeared to be. A lot of bellies hung over the old running shorts. *Piece of cake*, I told myself, confident I'd win.

Then the pistol fired. I took off . . . but something was wrong. I wasn't running like the wind! Those out of shape guys were passing me like I was standing still. I reached down deep for that extra energy burst that used to propel me on to victory—and while I did pick up speed, it was not soon enough to make a difference. By now I lagged well behind the other dads, and I was humiliated.

As I dropped toward the back of the pack, I quickly realized that not only was I going to lose—I was going to lose big. I could just hear the "token" applause that would accompany my stumbling across the finish line in last place. Not for me! I decided to cut my losses and drop out of the race right then. As I rounded the next tree, I sort of casually strolled off the track as if I really hadn't been a contestant in the Father/Son race. I had started the race well, but I finished miserably.

Contrary to what I had erroneously believed, the race was *not* a piece of cake. I learned that it would have been better if I had not been so overly confident. I hope to do a whole lot better in my spiritual race. However, I learned several things that day that I found I could also apply to the spiritual race all believers are involved in. First, I had to admit that I no longer had what I used to have! I hadn't trained for such a race. I had no current track record of consistency, endurance, perseverance, and runner's stamina. Most of all, my humiliating finish that day made me even more determined to finish my spiritual race, as I saw how easy it was to become discouraged and just drop out.

Not Everyone Finishes the Race

Sadly, the pages of the Bible are filled with those who fell out of their spiritual race, just like I fell out of the Father/Son race. These individuals may have had great potential. They may have begun to run amid much fanfare. But after a quick burst of energy, they flamed out. For some reason, they took their eyes off the prize and began to fall backward. Finally they failed miserably.

One of the things I appreciate most about the Bible is its honesty. The Bible is filled with many success stories, and I like that. Success stories are important. They keep us going. They pump up our hope. But the Bible is also filled with stories about real people—heroes, warts and all . . . and heels. For there are also stories about those who failed, fell short, and fell completely away. Because the Bible tells the truth, I find that I can learn something even from stories about those who fell away or failed. If I can see their faults and shortcomings, perhaps I can avoid making the same mistakes. Thank God, the Bible is an honest book about real people. Take, for instance, Israel's first king—Saul.

Saul was a man who had been given much potential. Instead of completing the race before him, he crashed and burned. Here was a handsome man with all the right stuff. He had God's blessing, anointing, and the makings of a really great leader. But, as Israel's first ruler, he was repeatedly disobedient to God's commands. He was finally disabled by constant pride and extreme paranoia. He summed up own life quite accurately when he said, "I have played the fool and erred exceedingly" (1 Sam. 26:21).

But facing the truth didn't change Saul's circumstances. He died a failure, and the kingdom passed to David instead of to one of Saul's sons. Saul had been given every blessing and advantage, but he blew it.

Then there was Samson, supernaturally strong and blessed by God in all that he did. He was single-handedly able to vanquish thousands of enemies. Yet he squandered his strength and potential by continually compromising. He exchanged his strength for sin, and lost it all.

Gideon is another man of humble origins who rose to greatness and fell via pride and immorality. Handpicked by God to lead the children of Israel into battle, Gideon and his men won great victory. But instead of living victoriously, Gideon dropped his standards, lowered his guard, and fell. While he had his moment in the sun, he spent the end of his life in the shadows of compromise.

One of these honest accounts about people who started well but finished miserably is the story of the Israelites in the wilderness. As you will recall, over two million Jews began the wilderness journey, which should have lasted three days but instead took forty years. Of those two million, only two individuals—Caleb and Joshua—were allowed to actually go into the Promised Land.

Lessons from the Life of Caleb

To me, Caleb is a classic example of a man who never lost his spiritual edge. At eighty-five, he was able to say confidently: "I am as strong this day as I was on the day that Moses sent me; just as my strength was then, so now is my strength for war, both for going out and for coming in" (Josh. 14:11). I imagine that gave many of Israel's young bucks a good chuckle when they heard aging Caleb make that statement. But soon they would see he was simply speaking the truth.

If Caleb were still around today, no doubt he'd have the leaders of the health and fitness industry scrambling for his endorsement. "Caleb, what's your secret? Is it a high-protein diet? What vitamins do you take? Where do you work out? Will you endorse our products? Will you appear on the next box of Wheaties? I like that—Wheaties, the breakfast of champions like

Caleb! That will really play to senior citizens! By the way, what's the secret of your strength at the ripe old age of eighty-five?" Imagine how shocked these individuals would be if Caleb replied, "Faith. It's faith in God's Word. That's all."

Faith is something Caleb never lost sight of throughout his long life. Caleb did enter into the Promised Land, and he was well able to take the land at eighty-five—just as he had been forty years earlier when Moses sent him in as one of the twelve to spy out the land God had given Israel. The faith he had at forty-five was the same faith he had at eighty-five. What an example for us today!

Where did this seasoned veteran, Caleb, get his spiritual grit—his *chutzpa*? What made him endure while others fell by the wayside right and left? The answer is contained in Joshua, chapter 14. Throughout, you'll find a phrase repeated that offers a glimpse into this hard-running saint's "trade secrets." I believe it is the secret of both his longevity and his spiritual stamina. The Bible says, "He wholly followed the Lord God of Israel" (v. 14). Another way to translate that would be, "He followed God fully."

I suggest to you that we will achieve the same results when we do the same today. We live in a period of history when the pressure to compromise has never been greater. Temptation is all around us. At times it is very difficult to resist. In times when we are pressed to compromise, we must continually remember that God will keep His promises.

Caleb never lost sight of those promises of God. They were ever before him, as he uttered a confession of faith at the entrance to the Promised Land. "I am as strong this day as the day that Moses sent me." Though his outer man was perishing, his inward man had been renewed day by day. He had maintained his first love, and that kept him from losing his first strength. We see the practical results of this inner strength demonstrated in Joshua 15:14: "Caleb drove out the three sons of Anak from there (the land promised to him). . . ."

Interestingly enough, of all those who received the Promised Land as their inheritance, Caleb was the only one who completely drove out the enemy. He faced some of the most formidable foes in the entire land. When asked which part of the land he wanted for his own, he asked for Hebron. Hebron was no garden spot. It was rugged and treacherous, containing a powerful enemy stronghold, guarded by the strongest men. It was no easy task to root out the enemy. But Caleb—even in his elderly years—was no lightweight. He wasn't looking for a pleasant retirement community to settle down in and rock his way toward heaven. He was looking for a scrap. He asked for one of the toughest assignments, and he successfully—and single-handedly, I might add—drove out the enemies from Hebron.

Perhaps Caleb had an ulterior motive when he asked for the land of Hebron. The Bible tells us that it was in Hebron that God spoke with Abraham face to face, giving him the promise of the land. The very name *Hebron* is descriptive. It means "fellowship, love, and communion." While others longed for Egypt, Caleb longed for Hebron—the place of "fellowship, love, and communion." While others looked back, Caleb looked forward. We can learn from that today.

Caleb's Keys to Finishing Well

1. No compromise allowed. The first quality we see in Caleb that caused him to finish well is his ability to stand his ground without compromising. In other words, he sought the approval of God over the approval of men. The Bible says, "Fear of man will prove to be a snare . . . " (Prov. 29:25, NIV). That is so true. We can become so paranoid about what others think of us that it paralyzes us. It will keep us from doing what God has called us to do. Caleb didn't worry about what his friends thought of him. He gave a good report of the Promised Land. He risked being personally ostracized by those who outnumbered him. He was willing to lose his friends, even his life, rather than turning back toward Egypt with the rest of the Israelites.

The Bible says that when the Israelites decided to follow the advice of the ten spies whose bad reports struck fear in their hearts, God was displeased and said: "Because all these men who have seen My glory and the signs which I did in Egypt and the wilderness . . . and have not heeded My voice, they certainly shall not see the land of which I swore to their fathers. . . . But My servant Caleb because he has a different spirit in him and has followed Me fully, I will bring into the land where he went, and his descendants shall inherit it" (Num. 14:22–24).

Since the Israelites had chosen to listen to the negative reports—even to the extent of desiring to kill Caleb and Joshua who brought back good reports, they spent the next forty years wandering around in circles in the wilderness, going nowhere. It was not that they were confused. It was not as if they had received bad directions. It was that God had sentenced them to wander because of their unbelief at the point of entry He had provided for them—Kadesh Barnea.

2. Take God at His Word. Caleb finished well because he took God at His Word. Despite this new setback of being sentenced to forty years in the wilderness along with his unbelieving friends, Caleb was fully persuaded that God would yet fulfill what He had promised to him. That's really something, when you consider that Caleb kept the faith in the midst of the whining, complaining, griping, and grousing going on among the other Israelites around him. He had to listen as they cried out for something more than manna to eat. He had to hear them beg for meat, and the garlic, leeks, and onions of Egypt. He was there as they rebelled against Moses, and he was forced to put up with that—and more—while he waited for God to keep His promise.

But Caleb remained faithful to God, and he received the promise because God cannot lie. We also must remain faithful to God, for as surely as we do, we will receive all He has promised. We will finish well.

3. Desire fellowship and communion with God. To do this, one must cultivate a relationship with God. When one maintains an intimate relationship with Jesus Christ, this world and all its temporary pleasures will lose its appeal. Caleb wanted fellowship, intimacy, and closeness with God. That vision is what sustained him through the hardest times.

4. Stay focused. We can finish well if we keep our eyes focused on the finish line. That means tuning out everything else. That means looking at the finish line only. No looking back. No looking around from side to side. No comparing ourselves to the other runners. No competition either. Just keep moving straight ahead. Caleb kept his eyes on the prize, and as a result, he finished well.

One day, as you round the bend, you'll see the finish line before you. You'll see Jesus there, waiting to congratulate you as you step across the line. What a great reason to stay in the race!

5. *Run to win*. Just as Caleb did, the apostle Paul knew our spiritual race was no "piece of cake." He wrote, "Do you not know that in a race all the runners run, but only one gets the prize? Run in such a way as to get the prize. Therefore, I do not run like a man running aimlessly; I do not fight like a man beating the air. No, I beat my body and make it my slave so that after I have preached to others, I myself will not be disqualified for the prize" (1 Cor. 9:24, 26–27, NIV). Essentially, Paul is saying, "I train. I discipline myself. I guard myself because I am not simply running to be running—I am running to win."

Paul could see the value of persistently moving forward: "Brothers, I do not consider myself yet to have taken hold of it. But one thing I do: Forgetting what is behind and straining toward what is ahead, I press on toward the goal to win the prize for which God has called me heavenward in Christ Jesus" (Phil. 3:13–14).

In this verse, he depicts a runner who has become tired. His every muscle is straining under the fatigue that accompanies long-distance running. Sweat cascades down his face. It drips into his eyes, temporarily stinging and blurring his vision. He wipes the sweat from his eyes, clearing his vision. Now he can see it! The finish line is in sight. That's the goal, just ahead! He's not looking around. He's not looking back. He's not going to drop out. He's not going to be disqualified. No matter what it takes or how much pain he's in, he's going to make it! That's what I want—don't you?

Paul used the racing analogy once again when speaking to the elders of the church at Ephesus: "None of these things move me; nor do I count my life dear to myself, so that I may *finish my race* with joy, and the ministry which I received from the Lord Jesus, to testify to the gospel of the grace of God" (Acts 20:24).

That's how I want to finish my race—with joy! I don't want to be overthrown by some self-imposed wilderness, as was Israel. I don't want to be listed as a casualty. I don't want to fall away. I don't want to be tripped up by the many compromises that the devil makes sure are presented before me. I want to cross the finish line joyfully—with flying colors.

It's Not Too Late to Finish Well

One of my all-time favorite films is *Chariots of Fire*. It's the story of two men who competed in the Olympics at the turn of the century. One of the runners—Harold Abrahams—was a dedicated young Jew. The other runner—Eric Henry Liddell—was a lightning-fast, young Scotsman and a Christian. In one of the most dramatic scenes in the Academy Award-winning movie, Liddell was preparing to run the race. As the starter pistol fired, he threw his head back, as he often did, and shot ahead of the pack. Suddenly he was intentionally knocked to the ground by one of his opponents. He lay in a crumpled heap in the center of the track as the other runners quickly distanced themselves from him. Many runners would have given up. Liddell, with a determined look on his face, rose up and began to run as hard as he could. Soon he was closing in on the other runners. In a dramatic, last-minute finish, he gave it everything he had. He inched forward, ahead of all the other runners, and won the race!

Perhaps you have fallen into compromise. Maybe you have gone down for the count. Are you tired? Discouraged? Do you feel like giving up? Do you fear that it's too late to start over and finish well in this spiritual race for the prize? You may think it's over. You may think, *I'll never accomplish anything for Jesus now. God could never do anything with a life like mine.* But I say that's not true. Get up! Start running! You can make it! It's not too late!

Jesus—your Intercessor—is seated at the right hand of God, cheering you on. He is your advocate. He's your Champion. He wants you to win. He wants you to finish well. How can you lose with Jesus in your corner?

For even if you have been wrestling with the guilt and feelings of failure that accompany great compromise, there is a way back to Him. He is ever merciful, faithful to receive you. He wants you to succeed.

LET'S PRAY

Jesus, thank You for being my Champion. Thank You for cheering me on to victory. You know how miserable I've been feeling—how I feel that I've blown it. But I believe You can help me out of the web of compromise that has ensnared me. I believe You can help me start all over again. Please forgive me. Put me back in the race. Cleanse me of the guilt and shame of failure. Make me a winner. Help me not only to start again, but to finish well. Teach me to study Your Word and to run with endurance the spiritual race before me. In Jesus' name, I pray. Amen.

EPILOGUE: YOUR INSURANCE AGAINST COMPROMISE

As I have already stated, the best insurance against *The Great Compromise* is a vital, sold-out, completely committed relationship with Jesus Christ. *He is your insurance against all types of compromise.*

Perhaps you've tried to achieve success completely on your own. You're self-made. You thought you'd be happy if you just attained promotion, obtained enough money, bought enough junk, or married the right spouse. But perhaps the bottom has fallen out of your self-made life. Your girlfriend dumped you. Your husband divorced you. There is still that void. So you step up your efforts to try and fill it. You try alcohol. Drugs. Now there's just more pain. You're losing it. Maybe sex will do it. You discover that casual sex only makes you feel more empty. All your illusions of being "a good person" have finally shattered to smithereens.

The Bible says we are all sinners. "For all have sinned, and come short of the glory of God" (Rom. 3:23, KJV). To think that we are basically "good people" and that our good works will get us into heaven is not true.

Then how does a person get to heaven? *By faith.* The Bible says, "The word is nigh thee, even in thy mouth, and in thy heart: that is, the word of faith, which we preach; That if thou shalt confess with thy mouth the Lord Jesus, and shalt believe in thine heart that God hath raised him from the dead, thou shalt be saved. For with the heart man believeth unto righteousness; and with the mouth confession is made unto salvation" (Rom. 10:8–10, KJV).

Jesus cares for you. *You* are the reason He endured the pain and the shame of the cross. Your sin has separated you from God. Jesus bridged the gap two thousand years ago, when He took your sin upon the cross and paid the penalty for you. No matter how good you ever hope to be, or how moral a life you lead, God's standard is 100 percent perfection—and no one can meet that standard.

Thank God, we don't need to! Jesus—totally man and totally God and totally sinless—did it for us. The Bible says, "While we were yet sinners, Christ died for us" (Rom. 5:8, KJV). You can have a vital, intimate relationship with Jesus Christ and God the Father if you will simply make Jesus your Savior and Lord. Jesus took extraordinary measures to reach out to you. Now He is ready to come into your heart and reside there. In fact, He has been preparing you for this moment: will you receive Him?

If you have never made Him your personal Lord and Savior, please pray with me:

> *Father, I come to You as a sinner and ask that You for-give me and cleanse me of my sins. I turn from sin now. I acknowledge that my own intellect and abilities will not get me to heaven. I also acknowledge that good works won't get me there. Only faith in Jesus Christ will save me. I place my faith in Him right now as I acknowledge that He is the Son of God, that He was crucified to pay the price for my sins, and that He rose from the grave on the third day. I believe that as He did, He conquered hell and death. Please help me to grow in the knowledge and understanding of Him and to apply His truths to my life. Jesus, thank You for the gift of salvation. Make me Your witness. Make me a winner in the spiritual race. Keep me moving forward, toward the finish line, and protect me from falling back or from being tripped up by the snares of compromise. In Jesus' name, I pray. Amen.*

ENDNOTES

PROLOGUE

1 W. Graham Scroggie, *Tested by Temptation*, (London: Pickering & Inglis, reprinted in 1980).

CHAPTER 1

1 Survey, "Why We Pray," LIFE Magazine, March 1994, 54.

2 Charles Colson, *The Body* (Dallas, TX: Word Publishing, 1992).

3 K. L. Woodward, "A Time to Seek," *Newsweek*, 17 December 1990, 50.

4 Jeffery L. Sheler, "Spiritual America," *U.S. News & World Report*, 4 April 1994, 48.

5 Susan Cyre, "Fall Out Escalates Over Goddess Sophia," *Christianity Today*, 4 April 1994, 74.

6 Ibid.

7 Ibid.

8 Ibid.

9 Elizabeth Mehren, "Stop That Whining," the *Los Angeles Times*, 4 November, 1992, E-1.

10 Ibid.

11 John F. MacArthur, Jr., *The Vanishing Conscience:* Drawing the Line in a No-Fault, Guilt-Free World (Dallas, TX: Word Publishing, 1994).

12 Henry Beard and Christopher Cerf, *The Official Politically Correct Dictionary and Handbook*, (New York, NY: Villard Books).

CHAPTER 2
No Notes.

CHAPTER 3
No notes.

CHAPTER 4

1 Warren Wiersbe, *The Strategy of Satan,* (Wheaton, IL: Tyndale House Publishers, 1988).

2 Alfred Lord Tennyson, *The Grandmother* [1864], published in *Bartlett's Familiar Quotations, 14th Ed.* (Boston, MA: Little, Brown, and Company, 1968), 654.

3 A. B. Simpson, *Christ in the Bible: The Epistle of James,* (Harrisburg, PA: Christian Publications, Inc., 1886), 9.

4 "Turn Your Eyes Upon Jesus," 1922, 1950 (Renewed) by H. A. Lemmel, assigned to Singspiration, Inc.

CHAPTER 5

1 Alan Redpath, from his book, *The Ten Commandments.*

2 Quote from Dr. Karen Hein of New York's Albert Einstein College of Medicine, taken from an article appearing in *The Honolulu Advertiser.*

3 "The Party," 1989 Queen Music/Beechwood Music.

4 Ibid.

CHAPTER 6
No notes.

CHAPTER 7
No notes.

CHAPTER 8

1 Bruce Frankel, "People Fear Losing Control," *USA Today,* 28 October 1993, 1A.

2 Michael Medved, *Hollywood vs. America* (New York: HarperCollins, 1992), 110; 112.

CHAPTER 9

1 Geoffrey C. Ward, *The Civil War,* (New York: Alfred A. Knopf, Inc., 1990), 271.

CHAPTER 10

1 As quoted frequently by Corrie ten Boom.

CHAPTER 11

No Notes.

CHAPTER 12

1 C. H. Spurgeon, *On Eagle's Wings* [*Morning by Morning*], (Bath, England: Creative Publishing, 1991), iii.

ABOUT THE AUTHOR

GREG LAURIE made a decision in 1970 that would change his life forever. He decided to commit his life and future to Jesus Christ. From that point on, he began to share his experience with others. Now, twenty-five years later, Greg's passion to reach the world for Christ continues through Harvest Ministries, a non-profit organization to which Greg donates his time and talents.

Harvest Ministries exists for the sole purpose of presenting the life-changing message of Jesus Christ to as many people as possible and to help believers mature in their faith. Harvest Ministries coordinates the Harvest Crusades, public evangelistic events known for their informal atmosphere, contemporary music, and simple, straightforward messages presented by Greg. To date, over one million people have attended these nondenominational events since they began in 1990. Harvest Ministries also produces a quarterly newsletter, *Harvest Fields*, and ministry tools, as well as the "A New Beginning" radio and television broadcasts aired nationwide.